AMISH LIFE
A Portrait of Plain Living

AMISH LIFE
A Portrait of Plain Living

John V. Wasilchick

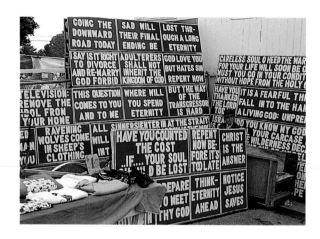

TEXT AND CAPTIONS: John Wasilchick

PHOTOGRAPHY: Jerry Irwin

DESIGN: Peter Bridgewater

EDITOR: David Gibbon

COMMISSIONING EDITOR: Andrew Preston

PHOTO EDITOR: Annette Lerner

CLB 2678

© 1991 Colour Library Books Ltd., Godalming, Surrey, England

This 1994 edition published by Crescent Books,

distributed by Outlet Book Company, Inc.,

a Random House Company,

40 Engelhard Avenue, Avenel, New Jersey 07001

Printed in Singapore

ISBN 0 517 06584 3

8 7 6 5 4 3 2

CONTENTS

INTRODUCTION

A consideration of how much the distinctive lifestyle of the Plain People has to offer our modern world

~

Strong families are typical of the Plain people. Grandfathers and grandsons enjoy the lively action of one of the many spring auctions that are important social events among the Plain people.

The traditional dress of Amish women contrasts sharply with that of their modern counterparts on the main street in Intercourse, Pennsylvania. The Amish in this community have tenaciously maintained their customs in spite of the presence of growing numbers of modern neighbors and tourists.

THE MODERN WORLD is constantly changing. It almost changes faster than we can keep up with it. Our world is becoming borderless as information, ideas and goods increasingly flow freely across political and ethnic boundaries. Advances in technology occur faster than we can accommodate them and make them useful. It took America several generations to replace horses with automobiles, a single generation to accept television as a part of family life, and just a few years to accept the VCR and compact disc player. The personal computer and the revolution in information it has made possible, have all happened since man walked on the moon.

Beyond the material benefits technology brings, what has been gained? In so many ways our modern world seems to be losing its ability to renew itself. Homelessness, illiteracy, poverty are not new to our world, but seem to be beyond our abilities to solve. The use of drugs and alcohol by children and rampant crime belie the failure of the modern world to convey values, basic beliefs about right and wrong.

In the midst of the seeming chaos of modern life are alternatives. It is hard to imagine a community that provides loving care for its elderly, and refuses Social Security; where there is no unemployment; where insurance is unnecessary because disasters are met by a community of neighbors ready to provide aid. The same community's children attend one-room schools, yet they are completely bilingual, mastering their German dialect and English.

This book will take you to communities where these occurrences are normal everyday events, and introduce you to the people whose faith in God and belief in hard work make this way of life possible.

This kind of community is not a far off ideal, but a close at hand reality. The Plain people – Amish, Mennonites and Hutterites – live in communities like these all across North America. The earliest Old Order Amish settlement is just 65 miles from Philadelphia, the largest settlement is in Ohio, not far from Cleveland. There are Hutterites in five states and the Canadian provinces of Alberta, Manitoba and Saskatchewan. These are people with strong values and firm beliefs. They communicate these values and beliefs not just through words, but through their way of life. They have chosen to live their lives apart from the modern society, rejecting much of contemporary culture as unnecessary, and against the spirit of their world.

The Plain people have maintained their way of life independent of the mainstream of the modern world, and without government

Horse-drawn farm machinery is still the rule for many Plain people who have rejected the use of tractors in the field as too modern and worldly. A team in the field hitched to a planter is a sure sign of spring in every Plain settlement.

aid or subsidy, for almost 300 years. The Amish and Mennonites came to the United States seeking the freedom to live and worship in their own way almost 100 years before the nation itself was born. The Hutterites arrived in the 1870s for the same reason.

The Plain people are distinctive because of their plain dress and distinctive customs. The men wear beards and wide-brimmed black hats, and the women cover their heads and often wear aprons. The Amish and some Mennonites do not own or drive cars, or use electricity on their farms. The Hutterites live a truly communal life, without private property or belongings. All still speak a dialect of German in their homes, and remain steadfast to the principles of their Christian Anabaptist faith that led to the persecution of their ancestors in Europe.

Too often the symbols of this distinctive way of life are confused with what the symbols stand for. It takes more than plain clothing and a horse and carriage to be Plain, and there are few converts to this way of life. Beyond the symbols of beard, carriage and hat is a way of life that has sustained itself for over four hundred years.

Because of their conservative dress and other customs, many misinterpret the Plain people as old fashioned, as examples of the way things used to be. The Plain people are not a reminder of what once was, but a clear statement of how a community of people have been successful in creating and maintaining a way of life – a way of life that has proven over time to be right for them. The Plain people give the modern world a clear example of how a strong faith can provide in ways the modern world seems to have forgotten.

Early summer brings a fresh crop of strawberries from the garden. The family garden is an important part of Plain family life, and produces most of the vegetables for the family table.

It would be a mistake to view the Plain people nostalgically or sentimentally. Theirs is not a way of life that is dying or will soon be lost. The communities visited in these pages are vital and growing. Increased contact with the modern world, rather than threatening assimilation, has made the Plain people more steadfast. These communities are prosperous and lively, rooted in faith in God, family, tradition and hard work. Life is simple in material things, but rich in faith and humanity. "Fear God, love work," is how an Amish farmer in Lancaster County summed up his approach to life.

There is much to be learned and rediscovered by the modern world from the Plain people.

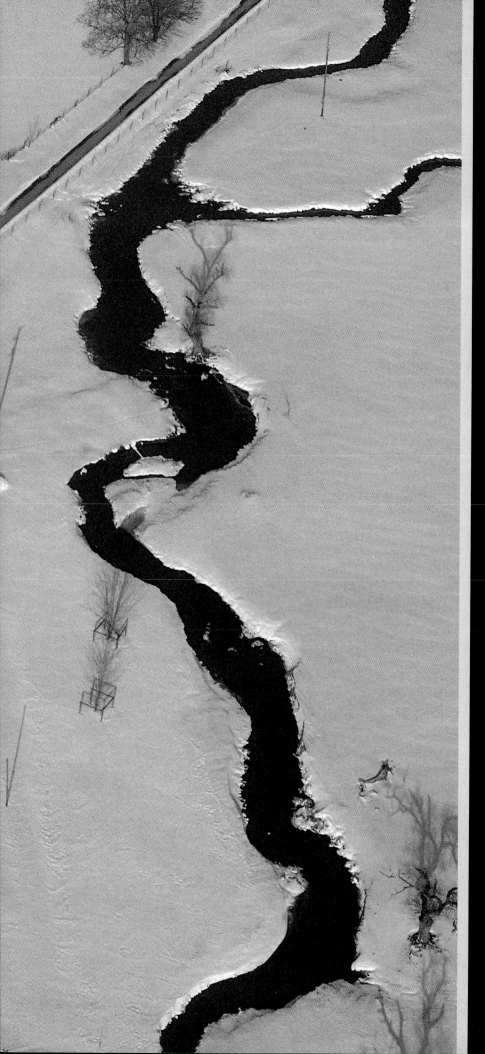

CHAPTER ONE

FROM THE REFORMATION TO THE NEW WORLD: A BRIEF HISTORY

The progress of the Plain

People from their roots in the

Anabaptist Movement of the

16th-century Reformation to

their settlement in

North America

~

Winter tranquility falls over
this Amish dairy farm,
typical of the many family
farms in Lancaster County,
Pennsylvania.

An Amish farmer comes to town in New Bedford, Ohio, deep in the Amish country of Holmes County. The Holmes County settlement was founded in 1808, and is currently the largest Amish settlement.

Wₕₐₜ ₐₛ ₐₜ ₐbₒᵤₜ these people we know as Plain people that sets them apart? Some of their customs make them immediately recognizable. Their plain dress sets them apart, and in the case of the Amish and some Mennonites, their preference for horse and carriage over the automobile also make them stand out. But how did this come about? And why have the Plain people steadfastly maintained their customs, such as dressing plainly, and why do they place such importance on it?

A large part of the answer lies in the traditions of these people observed over many generations, and much of their tradition is rooted in their faith. To begin to understand the reasons why these people have decided to live apart from the world, and reflect this in their dress and other customs, we need to understand their faith.

FAITH

The religion of the Plain people, the basis of their faith, begins in sixteenth century Europe with the origins of Protestantism and the Reformation.

In 1517, in the German city of Wittenburg, a priest named Martin Luther publicly expressed his dissatisfaction with the Catholic Church, and began a wave of protest now known as the Reformation. The Reformation ended the Catholic Church's monolithic role as the Christian Church throughout Europe, and established Protestantism as a permanent part of the Christian faith.

Zurich, Switzerland quickly became a center for the Reform movement. The environment of change was leading many to re-examine their faith, and within several years many had become dissatisfied with the pace of reform. This dissatisfaction boiled over in Zurich, when a group of Protestant Pastor Ulrich Zwingli's students began to criticize Zwingli and the Zurich City Council for continuing to baptize infants and conduct Mass.

The Zurich City Council would have none of it. After several heated debates with the Council, the dissidents were forced to meet secretly in private homes. On January 21, 1525, meeting in a home, a group of the dissenters secretly and illegally rebaptized each other. This action gave life to a new movement within the Protestant Reformation. Adherents to the movement were nicknamed *Anabaptists*, or "rebaptizers" by their Reform and Catholic contemporaries. The Swiss dissidents called themselves the "Brethren."

The Anabaptists believed that baptism should only be conferred on adults who were willing to discipline their lives, and live in total obedience to the teachings of Jesus Christ. Church membership conveyed through adult baptism was an individual commitment, a personal choice. The true church would not have universal membership administered through the baptism of all as infants.

They objected to the Mass because they felt the state church, even when it was a Reform church, used the Mass to keep the people spiritually illiterate. The Anabaptists based their faith directly on the scriptures, the words and teachings of Jesus. For the Anabaptists, ritual ceremonies on the Sabbath did not bring believers closer to "following Christ in life" or expressing their faith in their everyday lives.

The Swiss Brethren preferred the example of the early Christian Church, a community of believers who based everything on faith and obedience to the teachings of Christ. The Anabaptists took the Sermon on the Mount as their code. They renounced oaths, reveling and drunkenness, the use of force in war or civil government, and personal adornment.

The horse and buggy of a "Nebraska" Amish family climbs a steep hill near Barrsville, Pennsylvania. The Nebraska Amish are among the most conservative of Amish groups.

An Amish boy marries a Mennonite girl and will not follow in the family faith. There will be no sanctions or Meidung placed on him because he has not yet joined the Church. His family wears traditional Amish clothing.

By 1527, early leaders of the new movement articulated their convictions in a document now known as the *Schleitheim Confession of Faith*. Among other issues, these leaders committed themselves to literal obedience to the teachings of Christ, and the absolute authority of the New Testament as a model for their everyday lives. They viewed the church as a community of believers, socially apart from the evil world. It set forth a principal of nonviolence. This document is also the first articulation of the practice of denying communion to errant members, even to the point of ostracizing them from normal social relationships with other church members.

PERSECUTION

When the young reformers rebaptized each other in Zurich, they did more than just break with the Reform Church. They defied the civil authority of Zurich, and in so doing questioned the authority of the government to interpret and set church practice. This was viewed as a radical step, even in areas where the Reform Church had replaced the Catholic Church. The early Reformation had removed the Catholic Church from its status as the sole voice of Christendom, but it had done little to alter the political relationships between state and church.

The civil authorities and the Reform Church did not stand idly by while their authority, and the doctrine that supported it, was challenged. The response of the government and the Reform and Catholic Churches to these advocates of a new way of viewing the world was swift and bloody. Within five months of the first rebaptisms in Zurich, the first Anabaptist was executed for sedition. The nonviolence preached in the Sermon on the Mount was soon tested as the Brethren were forced to flee for their lives, pursued as "heretics." The Anabaptists' meetings were driven underground, and had to be held clandestinely, often in the forests or caves.

Life for the Anabaptists must have been truly grim, and their faith severely tested. Engravings from the period show Anabaptists being thrown out of boats into Lake Geneva. Their tormentors, other "Christians," gave them three opportunities to give up their belief in rebaptism or drown. Other engravings show public burnings and other forms of torture. Bounty hunters were commissioned to track down the Anabaptists and bring them to justice. Justice often meant being beheaded or burned at the stake.

Over the next two hundred years, thousands of Anabaptists would be killed because of their beliefs. The cruel persecution and the example of the martyrs remains an important part of the faith of many modern Anabaptists. A chronicle of the brutality, *Martyrs Mirror*, can be found in most Amish, and many Hutterite and Mennonite households. It is included in school lessons, and is often referred to in church. The back of the *Ausbund*, the Amish prayer book, also contains stories of the sacrifices and suffering.

DIASPORA

In spite of the waves of persecution, the Anabaptist faith was quickly spreading to other parts of Europe. It was spread not only by the flight of believers to friendlier lands, but by the missionary zeal that existed among the Anabaptists at this time. Many Anabaptists found refuge from persecution in Moravia, Alsace, the Palatinate and the Netherlands.

The grave of a thirty-two-year-old Nebraska Amish man is adorned with plastic flowers, perhaps left by a non-Amish neighbor. Flowers are seldom seen on Amish graves, especially those of the ultra-conservative Nebraska group.

For some the diaspora continues. This father and his sons are members of the Bardon Creek settlement in Belize, established by Plain people in search of a "pure Christian community" away from the temptations of the modern world.

They found sanctuary wherever the ruling nobility would allow them to practice their faith. Often their safety was only temporary. Succeeding noblemen were not always as tolerant as their predecessors. Circumstances changed as the political and military fortunes of the nobles changed.

Most noblemen in south central Europe at this time were consumed by war with each other, or with the Turks. Fighting for their lives against determined enemies now led nobles who had welcomed the Anabaptists to impose taxes on them to pay for their wars, and to conscript the men into their armies. Towns and farms were often pillaged by the local nobleman's army, and many Anabaptists were taken as slaves by the Turks.

Rather than compromise their religious convictions the Anabaptists were forced to move on. Service in any army, even forced, was against their commitment to nonviolence, as were taxes to pay for others who would wage war. Their only alternative was to leave or, in all too many tragic cases, to be killed either by their hosts or the invaders.

Among the earliest Anabaptists were some of the finest minds of the time. Their number included many very capable people from various walks of life. Intellectuals, priests, artisans, merchants and others seeking to go beyond what the Reform Church offered were drawn to this new belief. Many were offered refuge from persecution because of their skills as physicians, printers, smiths, paper makers or some other sought-after talent.

A small bird that has fallen from its nest has found help in the hands of a young Mennonite girl.

As the rebaptizers fled from persecution, a gradual transformation took place, not only in their physical location, but in their occupations, and how their communities were organized. Many turned to farming and sought refuge in the more mountainous regions, or in remote rural areas away from their enemies, where they could live in peace and practice their faith. This geographic isolation furthered their social distance, as they sought to live apart from what they saw as the evil world. Just as their churches were organized as covenants of true believers, their communities became more closed to "the world." Soon the Anabaptists were living in primarily agricultural communities, set off from the mainstream, and dealing with the rest of the world as little as possible.

Ultimately, the Anabaptists (who would become the Plain people) would escape to North America, but not until some had passed through many other parts of Europe including the Netherlands, Germany, France, and Russia.

THE EMERGENCE OF THE MENNONITES, HUTTERITES AND AMISH

Europe at this time was exploding with change, not only in religious thought, but in trade, science and art. It was change fueled by the rush of ideas and intellect produced by expanding trade, and the new world of knowledge created by the Renaissance. Just as the world was being redefined by the discovery and exploration of the New World, the reform movement was redefining the possibilities of the relationship between man, church and God. If it appears now that the world of sixteenth century Europe had been stood on end, imagine how it must have appeared to those who were part of the change.

After a sunup until sundown day of helping with the wheat harvest, an Amish boy lingers in the field for a few minutes of play before returning home.

MENNONITES

By 1531, the change had reached a young Catholic priest in the Netherlands named Menno Simons. He had begun to doubt his church's doctrine of the Mass as well as infant baptism. Seeking answers to these doubts he turned to Biblical study. This led him closer and closer to the simplicity of the new Anabaptist beliefs. Finally, in 1536 Simons left the Catholic Church and joined the house-church movement of the Anabaptists in the Netherlands.

Simons became a dynamic leader of this new faith in the Netherlands. He organized underground house-church groups, preached, debated, taught and wrote extensively. He was an important advocate for

Hutterite colonies employ huge grain combines to harvest up to 10,000 acres of grain. The machines, like everything else, are part of the communal property that make Hutterite life unique.

Hutterite girls offer fresh vegetables for sale at a farmer's market in the city park of Maple Creek, Saskatchewan. The small polka dots on their scarves indicate that these girls are members of a Dariusleut colony.

what he believed were the simplicities and directness of the teachings of the Bible, and a forceful spokesman against what he called the "legends, fables, holy days, images, holy water, confessionals, pilgrimages, vespers and offerings," that the state church fed to the common people. Simons' leadership was so influential that Anabaptists in Northern Europe became known as *Mennoists* or Mennonites. Eventually, almost all Anabaptists would come to be known as Mennonites.

The Mennonite faith today has many varieties, and among them are the Plain people, known generally as Old Order Mennonites. Thése Plain people have their origins in Switzerland and Germany. As has been mentioned, they are easily distinguished by their plain clothing, simple life style, and in some cases by their horse-and-buggy culture.

Many divisions among the Old Order Mennonites have given rise to distinctive, local groups. Most have simple meeting houses for worship, while some maintain the practice of worshipping in private homes. A few Old Order groups do not allow the use of automobiles, while some do. Still others, like the "Black Bumpers," are allowed automobiles, but only if the entire car is black, including the parts that are normally chrome plated. The Mennonites who maintain the plain traditions today live in Pennsylvania, Virginia, Ohio, Indiana, Missouri and Ontario.

HUTTERISCHE BRUDERHOF

Moravia had become a haven for many Anabaptists who fled there from Switzerland, the Tyrol, Austria and other areas. Many local Moravian nobles were Protestant and tolerant of the dissenters. The congregation living in the Austerlitz area became divided, and in 1533 Jakob Hutter was summoned from his congregation of Anabaptists in the Tyrol to arbitrate. Hutter emphasized absolute obedience to God and denial of self will and private property. This denial for Hutter meant following the example of the early Christian church, and having a community of goods – a true, Christian communism.

Hutter proved to be not only a forceful leader, but a tireless organizer. He brought cohesive, decisive communal organization to the group, and became recognized as the *Vorstehler*, or chief elder. Hutter established a *Bruderhof* organization for living. This community of believers became known as the *Hutterische Bruder*, or Hutterite Brethren.

During a crackdown on religious dissent in Moravia by the Catholic priests, the members of Hutter's community were driven into the fields and forests. Hutter was captured, and he was subjected to several forms of severe torture, including the rack and whipping. On February 25, 1536, brandy was poured over his body and he was burned before the public in the town of Innsbruck. He died without revealing the identity of any of the members of his congregation, a martyr to his faith.

What makes Hutter's accomplishments astonishing is that he laid the foundation for the next four hundred years of faith and communal life, and he did it all in only three years. While it was left to succeeding leaders to continue and guide the movement, the initial teachings of Hutter, and the foundation he laid for the Bruderhof, are still serving the Hutterites in North America.

The political tension in Moravia subsided, and repression of the Hutterites eased as Protestant noblemen reasserted authority over their lands. The Hutterites entered what they refer to as their Golden Age, which lasted from about 1550 until approximately 1600.

During this time the Hutterites established over one hundred Bruderhofs and are estimated to have had between 20,000 and 30,000 adherents. Bruderhof schools were opened and a pattern for education established. A standard of internal discipline for the Bruderhof was set and missionary activities resumed.

The Golden Age began to draw to a close in 1593 as war again broke out between Turkey and the Hapsburg Empire that included Moravia. The pacifist Hutterites endured severe oppression. Soldiers were quartered in their colonies, depleting resources and disrupting the simple communal life of the Bruderhof. Many colonies were overrun by the Turks and their allies. Members were murdered or taken away to Turkey or other Ottoman territories as slaves.

Events after the war with Turkey brought no relief. The Hutterites were under constant pressure and persecution. First, they were caught in the fighting of the Thirty Years War, fought largely on religious grounds – Catholic against Protestant. This was followed by the Counter-Reformation, an attempt by the Catholic Church and Catholic states to retake ground, and souls, lost to the Protestant Reformation. During this period the pacifist Hutterites suffered as much at the hands of Catholic priests as from warring armies.

The Hutterites fled to the Slovaka region, (now northern Hungary), Transylvania, Wallachia, (now a part of southern Romania), and then, in 1770, to Russia. They settled in Russia first in Vischenka, and finally on crown lands near the German-speaking Mennonite settlement in Molotschna. During these nomadic times, the Hutterites fell away from the practice of communal living, but had managed to maintain the other elements of their religion as well as their ethnic identity.

After settling in Molotschna, two groups returned to communal living under the guidance of elders Michael Waldner, a blacksmith

A Hutterite child from the Pincher Creek, Alberta, colony dressed in the colorful traditional clothing of everyday life. The clothing of most Plain children mirrors that of the adults.

(*schmied* in German), and Darius Walter. Today the descendants of these two original groups are known as *Schmiedeleut* and *Dariusleut*.

When Russian became the mandatory language in all schools in the 1860s, and military service was made mandatory in the 1870s, the Hutterites, as they had so often in the past, began to prepare to move rather than compromise. Serving in the military was against their Christian beliefs in nonviolence, and they could not bring themselves to educate their children in a language that was not German, the language that remains the language of Hutterite worship. In 1873, representatives were sent to explore settlement possibilities in America, even meeting with President Grant.

In 1874, the Schmiedeleut and Dariusleut groups of Hutterite Brethren migrated to South Dakota. In 1877, thirteen families under the leadership of Jacob Wipf left Russia, and upon their arrival at Elmspring Colony in South Dakota, began to live communally. Wipf was a teacher, *Lehrer* in German, and the members of this community, and all who have descended from it, are known as the *Lehrerleut*.

Some Hutterites migrated as individual families and settled in the same area of the Dakota Plains. They became known as the *Prairie Leut*, and over time lost their Hutterite identity. Most of these Hutterites eventually affiliated with local Mennonite groups. The last of the Hutterites left Russia in 1879.

Jakob Hutter's Bruderhof became the basis for a unique form of communal living based on a shared faith. The Bruderhof way of life has been guided since its origin by these verses from Acts: "And all that believed were together, and had all things common; And sold their possessions and goods, and parted them to all men, as every man had need." Members produce according to their ability and consume according to need. The Hutterite Bruderhof is perhaps the only form of communism that has withstood the test of time. It has provided an example of communal living, with property held in common, that has lasted over 450 years.

AMISH

The persecution of the Anabaptists rose and fell depending on the political climate, and often the attitude of the local noble and his successor. Many Anabaptists began to retreat to more remote mountainous areas where they could more easily avoid, or hide from, their persecutors. Farming as a way of life became increasingly important, because it was both a means of self sufficiency in these more remote areas, and a peaceful way of life close to God's earth. These small, isolated communities settled into a pattern of life and faith that became routine. Left behind were the religious and intellectual fervor of the early years of Anabaptism.

An elderly Amish man enjoys a lively conversation at a sale.

Amish children peer at the passing world from their perch in the back of the family buggy. The Amish doll, faceless by tradition, contrasts sharply with the modern triangular warning reflector required by local authorities.

Birthdays are highly celebrated by the Amish, and are often accompanied by a "shower of cards" from friends and relatives.

Right: an older daughter irons using heavy irons heated on a propane stove by the light of a kerosene pressure lamp. Ironing is a never-ending chore in large Amish families. No-iron synthetic fabrics were quickly accepted among the Amish because of the work saved.

Left: the setting sun reflects in the windows of an Amish farmhouse, marking the close of another day of farming.

In the late 1600s small groups of Swiss Brethren were moving from Switzerland north into Alsace, a region that is part of modern France. They settled in the area between the Rhine River and the Vosges Mountains. A controversy arose that reached boiling point in 1693, and would lead the Alsatian congregations to break with their Swiss counterparts. The key figure in this dispute was a young preacher named Jacob Ammonn.

There were several key issues in the dispute. Ammonn had begun new practices that he wanted incorporated into the Swiss Brethren church service. He proposed holding communion twice each year, instead of once as was the practice. He wanted to include the rite of foot-washing in the communion service as the Dutch Anabaptists did. Ammonn argued that foot washing should be observed in obedience to Christ's command.

There was controversy over other issues, such as the excommunication of liars. Another dispute centered on the salvation of *Treuherzigen*, Brethren sympathizers who shared many of their beliefs and provided aid during periods of persecution, but were not church members.

But the issue that was to tear the Swiss Brethren apart, as it had the Dutch Mennonites one hundred years previously, was *Meidung*, or shunning. The interpretation among the Swiss Brethren for the most part was that excommunicated members were banned from communion, but not from the community.

Ammonn preached a strict Meidung. Strict, according to Ammonn, meant that excommunicated members should be banned not only from communion, but from normal social activity as well. This meant, for example, that excommunicated husbands could not eat at the same table as their families. Ammonn would accept nothing less.

A minister named Hans Reist, a gentle-natured man somewhat older than Ammonn, began to speak out against what he considered to be Ammonn's radical views. Reist became the leader of those who rejected Ammonn's interpretation of shunning.

Ammonn began to travel throughout Switzerland and Alsace challenging his fellow ministers on these issues. Finally, he called a meeting of all the ministers in the town of Friedersmatt, in minister Niklaus Moser's barn. Hans Reist did not attend. Ammonn read a letter listing six charges against Reist, and promptly declared him excommunicated. Ammonn then began to challenge his fellow ministers on the issue of Meidung. He excommunicated, on the spot, those who did not agree with him.

The dispute was not without the rancor found in the clash of strong personalities. During the course of the dispute Ammonn called Reist an "apostate" a "sectarian" and a "rebel", while Reist labeled Ammonn a "blasphemer," among other things.

Ammonn continued his dogged pursuit of strict Meidung. Shortly after the dramatic barn meeting, Ammonn wrote to the Swiss ministers and issued an ultimatum that they either adhere to his "Biblical views" or be excommunicated. Ammonn might have been viewed as a young upstart by his fellow ministers, except for one disturbing fact – a significant number of believers agreed, or at least were so concerned about the issue of the ban that they gave some credence to his word. Ammonn continued to excommunicate everyone who disagreed with him as he traveled from congregation to congregation.

When the tide of controversy finally began to subside, Ammonn had severely divided the Swiss Brethren movement. In all, sixty-nine ministers in Switzerland, Alsace and southern Germany were drawn into the dispute. And twenty-seven of them sided with Ammonn, almost all of them in the Alsace region. These congregations became known as Amish or Amish Mennonite and became a distinct sect.

Later, efforts were made to reconcile differences when the Amish apologized for their harsh and hasty approach to the issues, but they never gave up their demand for strict Meidung. The rift never healed. Less than twenty years later, in 1711, when the Swiss Brethren and the Amish left Switzerland in large numbers, they refused to travel down the Rhine on the same ship.

War, political upheaval, social change and frequent persecution forced the Amish, and Swiss Brethren (as well as the Mennonites in northern Europe) to leave their homelands. They moved to other parts of Europe, and many ultimately immigrated to the New World.

The experience of the Amish living in Montbeliard and southern Germany were in many ways typical of the forced migrations. They first migrated to Austria. Their next move was made less difficult because they were invited to settle around Volhynia, in Russia, in 1783. The Amish by this time were firmly settled into an agricultural way of life, and had become known as exceptionally productive farmers. Local nobles in Volhynia were eager for the Amish to settle their lands and increase its productivity. This group of Amish was one of the last to come to North America, settling in Kansas and South Dakota in 1873.

The gently rolling hills of the Susquehanna Valley near Kinzer, Pennsylvania are plowed to follow the natural contours of the land.

Previous pages: Amish farmhouses stand out against the patchwork of freshly plowed and planted spring fields near Menno, Pennsylvania.

The new world offered the Anabaptists the freedom to practice their faith in peace. It also offered something else that, by the 18th century, was becoming an important part of Amish life – the promise of abundant land for farming.

Not surprisingly, the first Mennonite immigrants to the new world settled in Pennsylvania. Pennsylvania was founded by William Penn, a Quaker dissenter who had experienced his share of persecution in England. The first Mennonites arrived there in 1683, ten years before the Amish-Mennonite split.

These first Mennonites were followed in the first thirty years of the 18th century by several other contingents, including a group of Swiss Mennonites. They settled in the Pequea Creek area of what is now Lancaster County, Pennsylvania.

The peak period for Amish immigration to the new world in the 18th century occurred between 1727 and 1770. Records of the day show that the *Charming Nancy* was the first ship to arrive carrying

a large group of Amish. She docked in Philadelphia in 1737. By 1748, the Pennsylvania contingent of Amish was large and prosperous enough as a community to support a Pennsylvania printing of the *Martyrs Mirror*, the Anabaptist account of persecution and martyrdom still found, as mentioned, in most Amish homes today.

In the 19th century groups of Amish living in Alsace, Bavaria, and Hesse came to the province of Ontario, and to the states of Illinois and Ohio between 1815 and 1840. Congregations from Waldeck and Marburg arrived in North America around 1817, settling in Somerset County, Pennsylvania, and Garrett County, Maryland.

The Lancaster County settlement became the largest, and supported the settlement of other areas in Pennsylvania and other states. Today, it has been surpassed in size by the Holmes County, Ohio settlement, but it is still the most densely settled area of Amish population, and an important focus for Amish life. Lancaster County is also home to large numbers of conservative Mennonites who maintain plain traditions and are known collectively as Old Order Mennonites.

The Mennonite faith continues to be practiced around the world. It is recognized as a part of the mainstream of Protestant faith. The Mennonite church is divided into conferences, only a few of which are home to Plain congregations. Most Mennonites are part of the modern world, while those Mennonites who maintain strict standards of dress and behavior are referred to as Old Order.

Today, there are no Amish in Europe. Those that remained were not able to sustain their identity as a practicing faith. In many cases, the remaining members affiliated with local Mennonite groups. Similarly, the Hutterites as a faith and community exist only in North America. According to Hutterite tradition, only two families remained in Russia after 1879, but the Hutterite identity ceased to exist after the emigrations to South Dakota in the 1870s. By 1879, the Hutterite exodus from Russia was complete.

The success of these dissenting groups in their homelands can be measured as survival. From the caldron of the Reformation, through over two centuries of persecution and pacifism in the face of war, they were true to their beliefs and maintained their existence and identity. In the 18th century, the Plain people were able to establish roots in the freedom of the New World. And today their Plain descendants prosper and flourish.

Far left: farm animals are safe from the elements inside a barn on an Amish farm in the Conewango Valley of New York.

The sun rises over western Chester County, bordering the Lancaster County Amish settlement. The first Amish settled in this area in 1760.

CHAPTER TWO

DEFINING PLAIN
LIFEWAYS

How the distinctive

practices, customs and

traditions of the

Plain People are born out

of their faith

~

A barn door near
Sugarcreek, Ohio is painted
to resemble a traditional
Amish quilt. The quilt
pattern is known as the
center diamond and was one
of the most popular patterns
of past generations.

Amish schoolgirls pause on their way to school near Cashton, Wisconsin. The young "scholars," as school-aged children are often called, are wearing winter capes typically found in many Amish settlements.

THE AMISH, HUTTERITES and Old Order Mennonites have a common religious heritage in the Anabaptist movement of 16th century Switzerland and Germany. The faith and practices of the early Anabaptists in Europe are still the foundation of beliefs held by their modern descendants in the New World. The Anabaptists established more than a religion in the way it is commonly practiced by Christians. They believed in "following Christ in life" and expressing their faith in their everyday lives. This basic tenet still guides much of the behavior of the Plain people today, and is responsible for many of their distinctive customs.

UNSER SATT LEIT, ANNER SATT LEIT

The world for most Plain people can be easily divided into "our kind of people" and "the other kind of people" – *Unser satt leit, anner satt leit*. Our kind of people follow the path to salvation by living humble lives, obeying the rules of the church and customs of the community. The other kind of people, which is everyone else, are on the road to destruction. The world of the other kind of people is filled with temptation, where it is very difficult to live a proper life that will lead to salvation. It is a world of vice, vanity, competitiveness, ambition and pride. The daily flood of news concerning violent crime, drug abuse, the greed of business and politics, and other social ills confirms for the Plain people the rightness of the division.

This view of the world is also expressed in the desire of the Amish, Hutterites and Old Order Mennonites to live "apart from the world." In this context, the world means all that is not part of the Plain community. The world is what lies outside. Outside not only the physical boundaries of the community, but the moral and ethical boundaries as well. For the Amish, for example, the basis of this belief lies in the interpretation of biblical directives like that found in Romans 12:1: "Be not conformed to this world, but be ye transformed by the renewing of your mind that ye may prove what is that good and acceptable and perfect will of God." In a similar way, the Hutterites compare their colonies to the Ark of Noah. The world is divided into those who are in the Ark, and those who are not.

This view of the world that divides the believers from the unbelievers was furthered by the persecution experienced for generations in Europe. Separation from the world after arrival in the New World was not a difficult matter. The Plain immigrants established agrarian settlements in the relative isolation of new lands, in nations promising religious freedom. This allowed a measure of geographic separateness that reinforced separateness of their beliefs. This pattern of rural community living continues today, especially in new settlements and Hutterian colonies.

GELASSENHEIT

Donald Kraybill, a leading scholar and authority on the Amish has identified *gelassenheit* as a concept central to how the Amish understand their world. The same concept has been applied to the Hutterites, and can apply to Old Order Mennonites as well. Kraybill explains gelassenheit as submission, yielding to a higher authority. According to Kraybill, gelassenheit is also expressed in other values held by the Amish, like obedience, humility, thrift and simplicity.

The attitudes and behaviors embodied in gelassenheit are also a means of following the example of Christ. The activities of everyday life become yet another way to glorify God. "JOY" is an acronym used to remind and instruct small children about the importance of yielding themselves to their community and a Christian life. JOY signifies that Jesus is first, You are last and Others are in between.

Individuals who have been raised in an environment that nurtures gelassenheit seem subdued and humble compared to their individualistic, ambitious counterparts from society at large. Those with Plain values find fulfillment through their community, not

The buggy whip becomes a toy for this young Amish girl waiting for her parents to hitch the horse to the family carriage. The carriage's gray top is typical of the Lancaster County Amish.

Amish children plant field tomatoes as their father guides the team through the field. The Amish often grow tomatoes on consignment for local canners. The tomatoes are planted in much the same way as tobacco.

Top: the handiwork of an Amish chair-maker awaits the finishing stain that will be applied by hand by his wife or son. Just as it is on a family farm, every member of the family is expected to do their part.

Above: an Amish chair-maker plies his craft in Pocahontas, Pennsylvania.

An antique Amish quilt goes up for auction in Bird-in-Hand, Pennsylvania, and brings a record price.

through individual achievement. In a world often typified by "me first" attitudes, Plain values clearly go against the grain by placing family and community first. While many in modern society actively seek the fifteen minutes of fame that artist Andy Warhol has promised every person will have, Plain people deplore public recognition. Local newspapers seldom mention by name individuals from the Plain community who are recognized for some achievement because of the embarrassment it may cause.

Plain dress and conservative attitudes towards transportation and farming practices are part of denying selfish desires, and yielding to the right way. Professional occupations, advanced education and abstract thinking are not part of the Plain world because they may lead to arrogance and self aggrandizement.

The Plain people are pacifist. Gelassenheit is expressed through an attitude of non-resistance that forbids the use of force in social interaction. The Plain people are conscientious objectors and refuse military service. They do not hold political office, although they will participate in school board activities. They do not use the courts, file lawsuits or work as police officers.

Some individuals will never be able to get along with other individuals. While Plain people share the same feelings and conflicts all people do, silence and avoidance are often the response. Among the Amish, Hutterites and Mennonites, individuals cannot be overtly hostile or overly aggressive towards each other. It would be against church rules and violate the behavioral code of the community. It is unheard of for individuals to be openly hostile to one another – ever.

It would also be a mistake to assume that there is no place for self expression among Plain people. The Amish, Hutterites and Old Order Mennonites each are groups whose members represent a wide range of personalities. Self expression comes in the form of woodworking, quilting, and other handcrafts that have become recognized and valued for their artistry and craftsmanship.

Many others find opportunities for self expression through hobbies, cooking and farming. Artist Sue Bender, writing about her experiences living with an Amish family, tells of discovering that for many Amish women gardening is an important means of self expression. Both in growing large arrays of spectacular flowers, and practical as well as beautiful vegetables, Amish housewives express both their personality and their commitment to home and family. What is never found, however, is a boastful attitude or excessive pride that would make it seem that one individual has placed his work or efforts above that of another. This would not be acceptable behavior and would be thought of as worldly and unchristian.

There are many benefits to those who live in Plain communities and yield themselves to the group. Plain people know that no matter what happens, they will not have to face it alone. Mutual aid and assistance are readily offered, and disasters that occur to individuals are met head-on by the community.

Sometimes a "frolic" will be organized to accomplish a certain task. A frolic turns hard work, like threshing wheat, butchering beef or pork, or producing apple butter, into a day-long event that is a social as well as a work occasion. Men perform the hard physical labor with children helping while the women prepare large, delicious meals.

At times of death or illness friends and neighbors pitch in to see each other through the crisis. A natural disaster like a flood, or the loss of a barn or house to fire, brings the whole community together in an effort to restore the loss. Barn raisings are the most dramatic example, and one of the most recognized popular symbols of Plain life.

Gelassenheit is a way of living, a way of thinking about oneself and the world, rather than something overtly taught or learned. For those growing up in an Amish or Mennonite community or Hutterite colony, it is the natural way to view the world, and themselves.

THE BARN RAISING: HOLMES COUNTY, OHIO

On a Tuesday during the summer of 1988 over 1000 people came together on the Burkholder family farm in Holmes County to help raise a new barn. Only several days before, the old barn had burned to the ground in a fire started by lightning. Many of the Burkholders' nearest neighbors immediately pitched in to help clear away the debris left from the fire, and make sure that the chores continued to be performed. Dairy cows have to be milked, whether there is a barn over their heads or not.

One local Amish farmer was consulted concerning what would be needed to build a new barn. A full time farmer, this Amishman had supervised the construction of over 100 barns in the Amish community in Ohio, all without plans or blueprints. The new barn would be built under his supervision. The supplies were ordered and a date set for the raising of the new barn the following week.

Once set, the date was communicated throughout the Amish community. Preparations began to be made for men to contribute their time and energy to raising the barn. Alice Burkholder, along with her daughters, sisters and friends began to assemble the provisions necessary to provide large meals for the men at work.

Previous pages: weather is no deterrent to the sturdy horse-and-buggy Plain people. Often the horse and buggy is able to travel on roads closed to automobiles. A barn raising is the most dramatic example of the mutual aid that is a part of every Plain community. This barn near New Holland, Pennsylvania is being built in the old post and beam style with hand hewn lumber. The beams are raised by hand and joined using mortise and tenon. Overleaf: seven hundred men, from young boys to "grossdawdys" raise the Burkholder's barn near Farmerstown, Ohio. Work began at dawn and the barn was under roof by noon. Over 1,000 men, women and children enjoyed the noon meal.

Workers swarm as the Burkholders' barn begins to take shape. The barn will be complete enough by evening for the Burkholders to milk their cows inside.

A Mennonite hog farmer tends his livestock. With land prices soaring, many Mennonites adapt to smaller farms by specializing in hog farming, while many Amish have responded by concentrating on dairy farming.

They, too, would be helped by women from all over the Amish community. As part of the preparation, the Burkholder family would consult family notes from a previous work day twenty years before, as well as the wisdom of others who had recently prepared food for a barn raising.

The building materials would be paid for through the Amish Aid Society, an informal plan that pays for the replacement of property lost to fire or weather. A local volunteer director collects a fire tax from each family. The amount collected is based on the assessed value of the family farm. In this way the cost of recovering from a disaster like a barn fire is spread across the community. When the treasury runs low, the Society will instruct the directors to collect. Collection depends on the frequency of fires. Members from far and wide will gather and contribute all the labor and tools needed for the clean up and rebuilding.

For an occasion like a barn raising, many Amish businesses will close for the day to allow their employees to help. On the day of the Burkholders' barn raising practically every Amish business in the area was closed.

They began to arrive before dawn, and by six in the morning 1000 people were ready to begin work. About 700 men had come to raise the barn and 300 women to help cook and serve the hearty meals. Many brought chickens, hams, canned goods, and fresh fruit and vegetables from their gardens to be served.

The barn was under roof by noon, when the first workers began to eat dinner. And by six that same evening the Burkholders were able to milk their cows in the barn. The following Saturday wheat was threshed on the floor of the barn.

PLAIN LIVING ON A PERSON TO PERSON TO PERSON BASIS

One key to the enduring traditions and success of the Plain way of life is the scale on which it is organized. Plain life is to a great extent built upon face-to-face relationships established over time, often over generations. The scale of the Plain community is small and allows almost everyone to know everyone, or someone else who does. The small scale creates an environment of mutual interest and aid that enhances both social control and social integration. This environment makes it difficult to wander from the norm, and ensures that very few will want to wander.

The family is the key building block of Plain communities, and families are typically large. Nearby families are joined together into church districts. When the number of families in a district becomes too large for the small Mennonite meeting house, or more than an Amish home can accommodate for church, the district divides. Church units that share common practices are said to be "affiliated."

For example, the typical Amish family visits the home of every other family in its congregation at least once a year for worship. It is hard to stray too far from the fold when the fold will soon visit. What other contemporary institution brings its members together so closely? The small scale of life also means that individuals know who they are, and where they fit in their family, their community, and the world. Perhaps this explains, at least in part, the lower rate of mental illness and other social ills among the Plain people.

There is little bureaucracy or organization above the face-to-face level in the Plain community. Among the Amish and Mennonites, leadership outside the family is provided by the minister, and above the minister is a bishop. Each bishop is responsible for two congregations, and the Bishops in a settlement meet together as a

Amish women pause after preparing the noon meal to watch work on the Burkholder barn. They will soon be called on to serve the noon meal to hundreds of hungry men who have been at work since dawn.

group from time to time. There is no further hierarchy. In fact, neither the ministers nor bishops have any specialized training. They are called, usually by lot, from among the congregation. In a similar way, the one room schools are run in a direct and hands-on fashion by those whose children attend them, and the teachers have no specialized training. There are no official spokesmen, elected political officials, celebrities or higher authorities. There are family members, neighbors, fellow church members, other Plain people and "the other sort of people."

The small scale on which life is negotiated has not prevented Plain people from establishing relationships outside their family, church district or even settlement. As church districts have divided, daughters married, and families spread out in search of land, the network of relationships has spread out. Keeping in touch is an important activity in every Plain community.

The Budget of Sugarcreek, Ohio speaks to the need to keep in touch at a person to person level. *The Budget* is composed entirely of letters, and many of the letters printed each week recount the experiences and travels of Plain people as they visit relatives both close and distant and attend weddings and funerals. Even though these interactions may be as far flung as the Yoders of Dover, Delaware attending church at the home of the Bontragers in Chouteau, Oklahoma while in town to attend the wedding of their granddaughter, they are still conducted on a face-to-face basis, and within an extended network of family and church.

KEEP IN TOUCH

Plain people do not have ready access to telephones. Even if use of the telephone is permitted, it is usually located away from the home or limited to business use. And yet members of the Plain community have an uncanny ability to stay in close contact with each other.

Both *The Budget* and *Die Botschaft* play an important role. *The Budget* serves the entire plain community. *Die Botschaft* was founded in Lancaster, Pennsylvania, to serve the "horse and carriage" portion of the Plain community that prohibits ownership of automobiles. Both papers are composed completely of letters from Plain people.

The letters cover a variety of topics, and many include notes about family members or neighbors with special problems. Others with similar problems or experiences write to offer their advice, insights and moral support. A family with a child with a heart problem faces a long and arduous road ahead in dealing with the child's condition. After being mentioned in a letter to *Die Botschaft* or *The Budget* by a friend or relative, hundreds of cards and letters will arrive. Many will come from families with children who have

Young Amish boys plot their next adventure, and share their thoughts much as their fathers did a generation ago. The conversation in this huddle is surely spoken in dialect.

Top: children are a blessing from God for the Plain people, and twins doubly so.

Above: Amish and Mennonite farmers, and their children, bring their produce to market at Good's Auction in Leola,

similar conditions. The letters will offer the practical advice of loving parents who have experienced and are experiencing the same problems. The letters will include heartfelt encouragement and prayers.

These correspondences are important connections for Plain families and go beyond letter writing. Families who get to know each other through their letters will often have an opportunity to meet and visit from time to time. There is a built in network of support and shared interests for Plain people traveling during the winter months. Lancaster County families visiting relatives in another settlement will often spend a day with another Plain family with whom they share a special interest and have met through correspondence. For families facing a difficult problem such as a childhood illness, it is a special time to share problems and experiences with those who understand on a first hand basis.

Sometimes, when a person faces an unusual problem or illness, a letter to *The Budget* or *Die Botschaft* will ask for a card "shower". The individual will then receive a flurry of cards and letters of encouragement or condolence from all over the Plain community.

Circle letters are a popular pastime and an important source of information. The content of these letters ranges from the practical and informative to the fanciful. Some are to keep a far-flung family informed about all of its extended members. Some unite families or individuals around a common interest such as families with handicapped children, or childless couples. Farmers with common agricultural concerns will circulate letters as a way to compare practices and methods. There is even a letter circulated among women named Katie, for no other reason than they share the same first name, and enjoy the companionship the letters from others brings.

Through open letters in *The Budget* and *Die Botschaft*, circle letters, and the lively personal correspondence many carry on, Plain people are able to communicate and share special interests and concerns with others both close by and in other settlements. All, of course, within the understanding of what it means to be Plain.

THE SOUNDS OF PLAIN LIFE

One of the most distinctive aspects of life among the Plain people is its sound. Among the Amish and Old Order Mennonites there is the sound of the hooves of six or eight mule teams in the field. There is the sound of the hoofbeats of a horse pulling a carriage down a country road, and the whir of carriage wheels in areas where the automobile has been prohibited. For Hutterites farming on the great plains of the Midwest, there is the stillness of the plains

Dressed for church, two young girls wait for the team to be hitched up to take them to Sunday church service.

A young Amish boy learns to handle a team by using the roller to flatten and prepare the soil for planting. The family dog, a small white husky, comes along for the ride.

An Amish girl, dressed in typical everyday clothing, poses for a photograph. Young Amish girls often appreciate a photograph as a keepsake, knowing that after they join the Church pictures are strictly forbidden as graven images.

Previous pages: an Amish man with horse and cart is silhouetted against the sky as he travels a farm road at the end of the day.

heard early in the morning or late at night when the work is done.

But the most distinctive sound of Plain life is the conversations one overhears, the rhythmic patterns of lively discussions, the quiet conversations, – all in German dialect. Here in the midst of the largest English speaking nation in the world, whose economic might has helped transform English into an international language – are whole communities of people who speak German dialects. Dialects that are more like the language spoken 200 years ago than the contemporary German heard today in Zurich or Frankfurt.

German dialect is the native language of the Plain people. It is the language that children first learn at home from their parents. It is the language that Amish children speak at play in the schoolyard, and the language young Hutterite men speak at work in the fields. German dialect has been more than just a means of communication. It has served to define the Plain community and set it off from the "English," a term Plain people use to describe everyone who is not Plain. It is a clear and definite indication of *unser satt leit*.

Children are raised speaking dialect, and do not learn English until they enter school. There they are taught to read and write English, and by the fifth or sixth grade they are competent in both languages. In Hutterite colonies there is even a separation in teaching: English is taught in the English school from text books used in the public school curriculum, and German is taught in German school from Hutterian texts and the Bible.

English is more important to Plain people as a written language than a spoken language. All letters to *The Budget* are written in English, as are the Amish publications *Family Life* and *Die Botschaft* (contrary to what one might assume from the name, which means *The Message*).

English is spoken freely to non-plain neighbors. It is used extensively in shopping and interactions with strangers. But German dialect is the language of Plain life's intimate conversations, family discussions, work plans and social activities. When the young Mennonite and Amish men gather to play corner ball or *eck* at a farm sale – the score will be kept in dialect. When an Amish farmer in LaGrange Indiana, discusses the plowing planned for the day with his son, they discuss it in dialect.

There is another language important to each of the Plain faiths. It is known as "High German" and is the language of the sacred. It is the language of the Bible used in church services. It is the language of the *Martyrs Mirror*. Most Plain people are familiar enough with High German to read and understand the Bible, readings from *Martyrs Mirror* and prayer. It is not a conversational language, and is only used in a formal religious setting. It is taught at home as part of religious instruction, but the Hutterites teach it as part of the course of study in the German school.

The use of dialect provides an identity for the Plain community that sets it apart from the community at large. It helps reinforce the division of those who seek to follow Christ in life and are "apart from the world" from those who are part of the evil world. The German dialect also provides an important historical link with the past. It recalls the roots of the Anabaptist tradition, the formation of the Mennonite, Hutterite and Amish traditions, and the sacrifices of the early martyrs.

DRESSING PLAIN

Plain dress for the Amish, Hutterite and Old Order Mennonites is an act of faith and a tradition.

The roots of the Plain wardrobe lie in traditional European peasant costumes, early American customs, and the traditions that have built up in Plain communities over the years. Plain dress to those who have grown up with it and live in communities where it is common, is as natural as a suit and tie to an executive in New York or London.

The tradition of Plain dress is more than just a practice passed down over the years. It has come to stand for much of what the Plain people think is right about their world. Plain dress, like their farming practices, German dialect, strong family and faith in God, have sustained them through generations. To change would be to become worldly and put at risk not just a way of dressing, but a way of life.

Plain dress in this way shows the yielding of the individual to the common values of the group. Plain dress creates a common identity for the group, and clearly defines the Plain person relative to the rest of the world, as well as other Plain groups. This style of dress is part of being apart from the world. It reflects humility, commitment, and the willingness to be non-conforming to the evil of the world. It is consistent with the values embodied by gelassenheit.

In understanding Plain dress, what is not worn is as important as what is worn. All of the outward symbols of individual style and taste are missing in the Plain wardrobe. Jewelry is not worn, and there are no fashions to reflect individual style and taste.

Change and personal style do exist, but occur in subtle ways. The width of a hat brim, hair length, shoe color and hem length all communicate how conservative or liberal an individual is. In the past young men among the Amish in Lancaster County cut their hair very short to aggravate their elders, while today they let it grow too long.

Two changes affecting Plain dress in recent years are the use of synthetic fibers and sneakers, also known as tennis shoes. Single

Her knitted bonnet identifies this youngster as a member of the Wenger Mennonite group in Lancaster County. Her bicycle is another indication that she is from a Mennonite family, because bicycles are forbidden among the Lancaster County Amish.

and double knit fibers were quickly embraced by the Plain people as they became available at a price competitive with cotton and wool. The major attraction is the no-iron quality of the synthetic fabric. Plain families are big. Among the Amish, six or seven children is not unusual, and families among the Mennonites are often even larger. It should not be surprising that Plain households were quick to adapt, so as to reduce the burden of ironing clothes.

Sneakers first appeared on young people who began to wear them for comfort. The sneaker also became a means of expression. Where once all sneakers were black, many young people now wear blue, grey or brown. Occasionally, a yellow lightning bolt can even be seen flashing down the side of a sneaker, below the hem of a long brown dress.

Sneakers have increasingly become more practical, as the traditional plain oxford and high top shoes preferred by some church districts have become hard to find. In some communities even older members have begun to wear plain black sneakers because of the comfort and increased mobility they provide. Sneakers are an issue in some areas, permissible in others, and ignored in still others. They will always be an issue if they are gaudy or flashy in style.

The actual details of Plain dress vary widely from group to to group and rely greatly on local tradition. Among the Amish, for instance, a man's work coat will have buttons in Lancaster County, Pennsylvania, hooks in Holmes County, Ohio, or snaps in LaGrange, Indiana. The head scarfs of Hutterite women are always dark blue with dots. The dots are large if worn by a member of a Lehrerleut colony, Schmiedeleut scarfs have medium dots, and Dariusleut small. In a similar way, the aprons the Lehrerleut women wear are tied in front, Schmiedeleut are tied in back, and Dariusleut are tied front or back.

There are no absolute rules or universal practices in the details of Plain dress. The most important thing about Plain dress has little to do with clothing. To dress Plain is to conform to the local rule, the *ordnung*, of the church, and demonstrate a willingness to yield to the group. Plain dress expresses humility, and shows that individualism is being denied. It is also a way to be visibly apart from the modern world.

A thirteen-year-old girl visits neighbors across the fence.

White organdy aprons and caps are the rule for Sunday service for young Amish girls.

Fresh fields of alfalfa and clover make an ideal playground for young Amish children.

ORDNUNG

The way the world is ordered, the rules for the group, discipline, are all part of the *ordnung*. The ordnung is the traditional code of behavior, kept as an oral tradition, that guides the settlements of Amish, Hutterites, and Old Order Mennonites.

The details of the ordnung vary from church district to church district. It is the local rule that tells the Amish of Lancaster County that they cannot use tractors in the field, while in Somerset County the local rule allows Amish farmers to use tractors for harvesting while draft animals must still be used for planting. Members of the Reidenbach Mennonite Church and Wenger Mennonite Church, in Lancaster County, are often neighbors. The Reidenbach rule prohibits electricity, telephones and indoor plumbing, while the Wengers are permitted all three.

It is often described by the Amish as an "understanding." It is an understanding that has evolved over generations as local leaders have faced the winds of change in the world and their community. For the local members of Plain communities, the ordnung is an understanding they are raised with, and seems the natural course of life. For a young Hutterite girl, wearing a polka-dotted head scarf is what young women wear. It is the way the world is and should be.

Ordnung has played an important part in keeping Plain communities separate from the world. Many of the technological innovations that would have radically changed the way the Amish and Mennonites live have been dealt with through the ordnung.

For example, in many areas tractors are not allowed in the fields, but are used as power plants in the barn. This has forced families to continue to rely on horses for work and transportation. This, in turn, has limited mobility, and kept the community very localized. It has also kept farmers from overextending themselves by buying expensive equipment and then needing to farm more land to pay for the equipment, a common trap that cost many of their English neighbors dearly.

In other areas, where soil is less fertile, tractors have been accepted over time as a means to allow farming as a way of life to continue. Horses limit the amount of land that can be farmed, and where the amount of land required to "make the living" is more than a team can cultivate, the ordnung has often accommodated their use.

Hutterites attach a slightly different meaning to the word ordnung. Within a Hutterian colony or *Bruderhof*, the ordnung is the collected written rules and directives that the Elders have adopted by vote. For instance, proper dress is frequently a subject, but so are decisions to build new barns, or purchase new machinery. While

Plain men root from the sidelines during an "eck ball" game.

the term ordnung may have a different meaning, the concept of discipline and order in life and how it is lived is very much present.

The ordnung is important because it addresses both what one is expected to do, as well as what one may not do. It is expected that among the Amish all men will wear beards, but no one may own a television. And it just happens, without discussion or much thought. At the right time most young men grow beards without mustaches, and no one would think to own a television.

There are occasions when individuals "crowd the fence" or test the limits of the ordnung, usually experimenting with new gadgets. Among the Amish, these fence crowders will eventually come to the attention of the Minister, and the Deacon, whose role it is to enforce the ordnung, will visit the fence crowder and ask the individual to "put it away."

Prohibited things are not considered evil in and of themselves. It is the impact they will have on current practices, on family life, on the group, that make the Plain people very wary of change. It is not just the immediate effect of new technology and conveniences that concern them, but what other unforeseen changes might also be ushered in with it. What will come next is always a consideration.

Many new innovations pass into general use without becoming an "issue." The hand-held calculator can be found in many Amish households and shops, and has not attracted any attention, while the portable weed cutter is allowed, but has been the cause of much discussion.

Sanctions for violating the ordnung are only applied to those who have been baptized and are adult members of the church. With baptism and church membership comes a promise to obey the rules. Sanctions are not applied to those who have not been baptized and have not violated their promise. The most severe sanction among the Amish is *meidung* or shunning. Shunning bans the individual from communion and from normal social interaction with church members, including family members.

The ordnung is important for what it allows, what it prohibits, and what it does not mention. It sets the width of the hat brim, the kind of tools to use in farming, and guides many other aspects of Plain life.

Plain life is more than Plain dress, German dialect and barn raisings. It is a way one views the world, and one's place in it. It is a way of life that requires the sacrifice of much of one's self to faith and to the group. It is life on a small scale. It is a way of life that seems to be holding its own, in spite of the pressure placed on it in many areas by suburban sprawl, high land prices and tourism. Plain life is a life way that demands a lot from the individual, but returns the support and security that comes from belonging to family, church and community.

CHAPTER THREE

FAMILY LIFE

Exploring the home life
of the Plain People through
the family routine of
a typical day

~

Against the evening sky, this
farmhouse looks still and
calm. Inside most Plain
homes, sunset is just the start
of family activities such as
sewing, singing and
homework.

An Amish housewife helps collect milk in the dairy barn. Amish housewives often carry a heavy workload, including some farm chores, especially when the children are pre-school age.

As the Beiler family gathers around the breakfast table, they have already been hard at work for several hours milking the cows, feeding the livestock and tending to the chores that every farm family must perform. Breakfast will not begin until all are seated at the table. Elam sits at the head, with his wife Sarah and daughters Fannie, Rosanna, Rachel, and Sophie on his right, and his sons David, Elam and Ike on the left. Breakfast is a substantial meal and includes eggs, sausage, cooked cereal, bread and butter and apple butter, and a serving of shoo-fly pie topped with milk. The room falls silent as Elam leads his family in silent prayer. The prayer ends as Elam raises his fork.

The silence is brief and in sharp contrast to this busy morning – and every other morning among the Amish and other Plain people. Elam and Sarah Beiler were raised in the strong faith and traditions of their Amish community. They now raise their children in the same way.

Elam is the head of the family, but leaves all household affairs to Sarah. Among Plain people, it is said that the husband is in charge of the barn, and the wife is in charge of the house. And for Sarah Beiler it is a very active, lively house that is in her charge.

Sarah's day begins before dawn each morning. She is usually the first to rise at about 4:30 a.m. Soon after she is dressed and the stove in the kitchen is lit, she will wake her oldest daughter Fannie who will in turn help wake the rest of the children. The youngest children, Ike, two and Lizzy, four will be allowed to sleep until just before breakfast. David occasionally needs a little prodding. At seventeen, David is involved in *rumspringa* or the "running around" part of adolescence and spends many evenings with his friends, or courting. *"Geh shoffa,"* – "get to work," Fannie teases her brother as he passes through the kitchen on the way to the barn. Rosanna and Rachel, twelve and ten, are quick to dress and begin their chores.

Sarah, with Fannie's help, will prepare breakfast, pack school lunches and prepare for the day. Sarah's daily routine as wife and mother will be much the same as her mother's, and that of most other Amish and Old Order Mennonite women in the Lancaster County settlement for over 200 years.

The center of family life for the Amish and Old Order Mennonites is the kitchen. It is here at the breakfast table that the events of the day will take shape and be discussed. It is here, in the evening, that the children will gather to do their homework, read or just talk. In

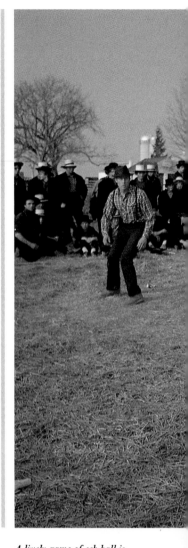

A lively game of eck ball is played at the Gordonville Fire Company sale and auction. Players at four corners try to hit opponents in the middle of the square with a soft leather ball.

fact, most family activities during the day will gravitate towards the kitchen.

And in Amish and Old Order Mennonite households the kitchen table must be a large one, because it will need to seat at least ten people. A typical Amish family will have at least six children, and among the Old Order Mennonites ten to twelve children is not unusual.

Sarah's kitchen is bright and warm. There is the soft, even illumination of naphtha "white gas" lighting in the early morning darkness, and the warmth of the sun through south facing windows during the day. The heavy, black, cast-iron wood-burning stove radiates warmth throughout the room.

Cleaning the milking equipment on a dairy farm is a chore that is often the responsibility of the girls in a Plain household.

Sarah uses a propane burning stove for cooking, but still prefers the wood burning space heater as a source of heat. Central heating will not be found among the Plain people. Her kitchen includes a propane powered refrigerator. The use of propane for cooking and refrigeration is permissible in the Beiler's church district.

Most Amish in Lancaster County can choose between wood, kerosene and gas stoves for cooking and space heaters, and can use some form of mechanical refrigeration. There are still some conservative Old Order Mennonites in Lancaster County that permit only wood burning cook stoves. The Nebraska group of central Pennsylvania and the Swartzentruber group of Ohio are among the most conservative Amish, and do not allow propane gas and have strict rules about refrigeration. Practices in other Amish settlements around the country vary with local tradition.

Most of the family's clothing – dresses, shirts and pants – are made at home, requiring Plain housewives to spend many laborious hours at treadle sewing machines.

Hand-rolled pretzels and spontaneous gospel singing, often in German dialect, are all part of a day's work for the Plain people who work at Martin's Pretzel Bakery in Akron, Pennsylvania.

Overleaf: bad weather is no deterrent when doing laundry for a large family. Wash can be seen hanging from the line at Plain households regardless of the weather every day but Sunday.

Conversation at the Beiler family breakfast table on this January morning concerns the events of the coming day. Farm life is a little less demanding during winter, and this is the season when Plain people spend time visiting and attending sales and auctions. Elam mentions that he has harnesses to mend, but that he might like to go to the sale of a nearby farm. Elam is interested for two reasons. He has an immediate need for two mules to add to his team before the spring, and he has a long-term interest in acquiring additional land that he can work along with his sons.

Elam is relatively young and a long way from retiring to the Grossdawdy house. While it has never been discussed, Elam knows that young Elam, now twelve, will someday buy the family farm when Elam and Sarah are ready to retire. David, at nineteen, will probably join the church and marry in the next few years, and Elam would like to help his son continue farming. Elam is proud of David. He has grown up to be a good worker, and Elam knows David is capable of running his own farm. Elam would like to buy another farm, and work both, allowing David eventually to take over the new one. Land is very expensive, and Elam is not yet prepared to take this step. But he will go to the sale and "get the lay of the land" for future sales of mules, and farms.

For Sarah, today is Sister's Day. It is the day set aside when Sarah and her three sisters who live in the area assemble to quilt, sew, bake or work together on some other project.

But first there is work to be done. After Rosanna, Rachel and Elam leave for school, Sarah will continue the work of running a large, active household. There is a never ending stream of clothes to wash and dry. Sarah often washes several loads a day. She has a gasoline powered washer, converted from electric power in an Amish shop. But dryers are considered too "worldly" and not allowed. She hangs clothes outside to dry every day that it does not rain, regardless of the temperature.

Without giving any thought to it, Sarah will hang her wash out in size order. Lizzy's small dresses will be followed by Rosanna's, Rachel's and Fannie's. The boys plain, black broadfall pants will be hung the same way, from the smallest size belonging to Ike up through Elam's. For Sarah, this order is an unconscious acknowledgement of the importance of tradition. Every day the Lancaster County countryside is punctuated by the solid blue and violet colored dresses and black pants and coats hung out to dry in size order, because "that's the way it's always been done."

There is cleaning to do, and Plain households have a reputation for being orderly and well kept. Fannie will do most of the cleaning for her mother while keeping an eye on Lizzy and Ike. Small children are never far from the example of work, and are encouraged to help. Work is often turned into play, and Fannie will find ways to include Lizzy and Ike in some of the fun.

The kitchen is always the source of wonderful smells and aromas as cakes and pies are baked, meat roasted, and vegetables prepared. Throughout the summer and fall most Plain farm families preserve the vegetables and fruits from their gardens through canning for use during the winter months. Sarah's cellar is filled with Mason and Kerr canning jars holding everything from string beans, beets, carrots and tomatoes to blueberry jam, apple sauce and apple butter.

The Amish are well known for their cooking, a culinary tradition they share with other German-speaking immigrants to Pennsylvania. This tradition is known as Pennsylvania Dutch. The name "Dutch" is a misnomer, and a degradation of the word *Deutsch* or German. During the early years of German immigration into Pennsylvania, their traditions, including their language, folk art and style of cooking became known as Pennsylvania Deutsch, mispronounced as Dutch. Over the years, the name Pennsylvania Dutch prevailed. It is a style of cooking that emphasizes hearty foods that will sustain people who are hard at work, and retains many German influences today.

Today Sarah is baking. She will bake bread for her family, "whoopee pies" – small cakes with a creamy middle, for the

Canning often brings together sisters, and mothers and daughters, as hundreds of jars will be processed at once. These women are at work in the "kessel house" area of the house, into which many chores spill over from the busy kitchen.

Top: a well stocked larder, the result of canning and preserving vegetables and fruit from the summer garden.

A Beachy Amish Mennonite girl pauses during her chores in her father's milk parlor.

children to take to school, and pies for dessert and as a treat for her sisters. Among the pies will be a "shoo-fly" pie, a pie made from molasses that is uniquely Pennsylvania Dutch. Sarah will pour and mix the ingredients not by measure, but by following her judgment. She began making these pies as a child helping her mother, and has never needed a recipe. She will add the molasses until "just so" and then the brown sugar until all the ingredients are mixed. Part of every Amish child's education is to learn by doing.

After a lifetime of experience, Sarah Beiler does not need to follow a recipe to bake her family's favorite shoo-fly pie. This recipe will make a shoo-fly a pie as good as any found in Lancaster County, Pennsylvania.

Amish women expect to work hard to help their husbands run a successful farm. Most Amish housewives are capable of running the milking operation when needed, in addition to their household chores.

SHOO-FLY PIE

LIQUID MIXTURE
¾ cup dark molasses. Dark Karo or sorghum
may also be used.
¾ cup boiling water
½ teaspoon baking soda

CRUMB MIXTURE
1½ cups flour
¼ cup margarine or butter
½ cup brown sugar

PASTRY FOR ONE NINE-INCH PIE CRUST
Into a 2 cup measure
pour ¾ cup molasses
add ¾ cup boiling water
add ½ teaspoon baking soda
and stir to dissolve
(the mixture will froth)

• Combine sugar and flour and cut in ¼ cup (½ stick) margarine or butter with pastry blender.
• Pour one-third of the liquid mixture into an unbaked crust. Add one-third of the crumb mixture.
• Continue to alternate layers, ending with a crumb layer.
• Bake at 375 degrees for approximately 35 minutes.
• The crumb mixture can easily be made in an electric food processor, although one would never be found in an Amish kitchen.

SISTER'S DAY

Sister's Day is a day for sisters to come together and help each other with their work. More importantly, Sister's Day is an opportunity for Sarah and her sisters to spend time together in a social setting, to keep in touch with each other while doing the work necessary to care for their families. An indication of the importance of close families and tradition are the many things that families pass down from generation to generation.

Many families pass down the patterns for the clothing they wear from generation to generation. Styles do not change, although fabrics have, and the patterns used by Sarah's grandmother are still in the family. When Sister's Day is devoted to sewing clothing the patterns will be brought out, and clothing for the children of all the families will be mass produced.

Colorful, intricate, decorative quilts are surrounded in most Plain households by plain walls painted in bland colors and simple furniture.

Recipes are also kept in families, not only the usual recipes for family favorites, but also the recipes and notes for preparing meals for the large gatherings of several hundred people who come together from time to time for a barn raising or a family reunion. When sisters gather to bake holiday cookies, hundreds and hundreds of cookies will be baked, enough for all the families of all the sisters, and then some, for friends and holiday visitors.

Sister's Day will be special today because Sarah's oldest sister, Becky, is visiting from her home in Ohio. This will be the first time all five sisters have been together since Leah, the youngest, was married.

Because it is Sarah's turn to host, she will choose the activity. Today the sisters will quilt. Quilting is a traditional handcraft practiced by Amish and Old Order Mennonite women. It is a skill that young girls learn from their mothers, and continue to practice through life. It is a skill that crosses age groups, and brings together granddaughters with their grandmothers. Sarah has a quilt top that she has carefully pieced. Placed on a quilt frame with batting and backing, Sarah and her sisters will spend their day stitching the quilted pattern onto the colorful one formed by the fabric.

Quilting is an important craft for Plain women because it is both practical and personal. It is one of the few opportunities Plain women have for personal expression, and yet, like most Amish crafts, it is functional and practical.

There is also a great demand among outsiders, the "English," for Amish quilts, and quilting has become an important cottage industry among the Amish and Old Order Mennonites. Many farm lanes along country roads in Lancaster County have homemade signs announcing "Quilts for Sale," always accompanied by a line of small print that reminds everyone that there are "No Sunday Sales."

Many women sell their quilts to shop owners in towns like Intercourse that are centers for the tourist industry, or through occasional auctions like those held in the small towns of Gordonville and Bart. The annual auctions in these small towns are held to benefit the local fire service, but are regularly attended by people from as far away as Washington, DC and New York City. Many attend specifically to purchase quilts.

Sarah's quilt is a traditional nine-patch block quilt, a pattern long associated with the Amish. The patches in the blocks are alternating colors of red and black in rows three by three. The background is a deep blue, a familiar color often used for dresses. This is surrounded by a broad border of black, with blocks of red at the corners.

Experienced quilters, Sarah and her sisters work quickly and will finish a large portion of the quilt in just one day. Sarah will finish the remaining quilting later, before once again getting out her collection of fabric pieces and beginning to piece together another quilt top.

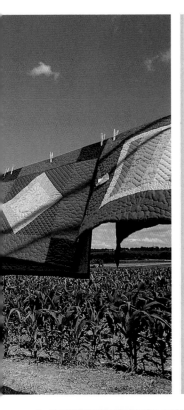

Above: eager bidders vie for an antique Amish quilt in the traditional center diamond pattern at a sale in Nickel Mines, Pennsylvania.

Many families offer their quilts and crafts for sale at roadside stands (above left).

Far left: a quilting bee that has brought together Plain women from several congregations in the basement of the Pequea Amish Mennonite Church.

Left: a quilt shop located in an early-nineteenth-century farmhouse near Bird-in-Hand, Pennsylvania.

Ascension Day is an Amish holiday, and the occasion for these Lancaster County Amish women to visit nearby Longwood Gardens. Botanical gardens and zoos are favored by the Plain people as recreation, while circuses and carnivals are disapproved of by most churches.

CHILDREN

Being raised Plain means growing up surrounded by the devotion and love of a large extended family. Grandparents and an unmarried aunt are part of just about every child's family. Most farm houses among the Amish and Old Order Mennonites have additions known as the "grossdawdy" house for the retired grandparents. Small children receive attention from relatives of all ages.

Plain people believe that babies are born good. Ike cannot be bad, and he is not disciplined. When he cries or is irritable, his family responds with warmth and affection. Ike and Lizzy are included in most family activities. Ike often plays on a blanket in the barn while his father works, or at his mother's feet while she sews.

The children living in Hutterite colonies spend the years from two-and-a-half to five under the careful supervision of several older women in the Bruderhof kindergarten. Here their play is combined with learning through games, songs and prayer. While the children are under the care of the kindergarten, both parents are free to work. Kindergarten was an innovation of the Hutterites in Europe.

By five years of age the example of discipline, respect and humility are reflected in the child's life. Children are proud of their small chores. Youngsters of five or six perform many, always carefully supervised by an older brother or sister. After breakfast Lizzy will help feed the ducks and chickens in the barnyard, throwing small handfuls of grain under the watchful eye of her mother or older sister. Even at play on the kitchen floor or in the barn, the lessons of thrift, cleanliness and order are demonstrated to small children like Ike and Lizzy through the example of their parent's work.

SCHOOL

Rosanna and Rachel Beiler, along with children from the neighboring farms, will walk a little less than a mile to school. There they will join other Plain children in a one-room schoolhouse, which is ideally suited to the needs of the Plain people. It is the best setting in which to teach cooperation, discipline and responsibility. There is no competition or comparison among the young "scholars," as the Amish call the students. Plain children grow up learning only those skills that will be useful and practical in their later lives as farmers, craftsmen and wives.

Children are taught English for the first time in school, although most first grade scholars bring a working knowledge of English to school. They are taught reading, writing and arithmetic as skills

Top: an Amish girl with a kitten for a playmate. Plain children learn to care for animals at an early age, often through the keeping of a pet.

This eight-year-old Beachy Amish Mennonite girl has mastered the hula hoop. Plain children often enjoy the same toys as their modern counterparts.

A group of young "scholars" before the class in a typical one-room school near Ephrata, Pennsylvania.

A young Amish Mennonite girl is dressed for evening Bible study. Young girls wear caps only for special occasions until they reach the age of thirteen, when the prayer cap will be worn as a part of their everyday dress.

One of this Amish boy's
chores is the care of a young
spring lamb. He may also be
responsible for other chores,
such as feeding the calves or

that are needed to carry on business successfully. Amish and Mennonite children learn High German in the last year or two of school. This third language is important because it is the language of the Amish and Mennonite church sermon and Bible. Hutterite children attend German school each day before attending their public school classes. Here they are taught by a Hutterite teacher and learn German through song, prayer, rote exercises and copying texts. Rosanna and Rachel are already familiar with many words and the sounds of High German because Elam often reads aloud from the family Bible.

The Beiler children, along with the other children of this Plain community, are educated by teachers who have no formal training, beyond that received in a similar one-room schoolhouse and an apprenticeship to an experienced teacher. The teacher instructs by example as well as through lessons.

The Beiler children's school is attended by Amish and Old Order Mennonite children. Children go to the Plain school closest to their home. The schools are built, operated and paid for by the parents, usually on a small plot of land donated by a local farmer. The school board is composed of local parents who are chosen to oversee the school's operation. Parents are intimately involved with the schools. Elam, along with other parents, rebuilt and shingled the school roof last summer. Sarah has helped on more than one occasion when the teacher was sick. The children also help out on a day-to-day basis by fueling the wood or coal furnace and helping to keep the building orderly and clean.

Each day at Rosanna and Rachel's one-room school begins with the Lord's prayer and a Bible reading. Religion is not taught at school because it is the family's responsibility to teach their children the Bible and the beliefs of their faith. While the one-room school does not teach about religion or God, the values of the community are taught and expressed in every activity.

One-room parochial schools, like the one attended by the Beiler children, are the rule in most Plain communities, but it was not always this way. In Lancaster County, Plain children attended public schools as long as they were small and local. When consolidations threatened to transport Plain children to large, regional schools, the Amish and Old Order Mennonites withdrew their children and established their own schools. In Kansas, and some other states with large rural populations and small local schools, Plain children still attend publicly-operated schools. In Hutterite colonies in Canada, the colony provides the school building, materials and a residence for the teacher, and the Province assigns and employs the teacher.

Formal education ends with the eighth grade for Plain students. For the Plain people, the goal of education is to prepare their

Plain families often host inner-city children through the Fresh Air Program. Facing page: a city friend joins in the fun of gathering ducklings, and proudly poses in her prayer cap just before leaving for church services.

Mennonite boys perch on a cart made by their father; a long line of Amish children push their scooters homeward after school; and an Amish mother, with boys in tow, heads to the house to clean up after finishing barn chores.

children to earn an honest living and lead a Christian life. Too much education is unnecessary and worldly. There is also the conflict between much of what is taught in public schools and the beliefs of the Plain community. Evolution, sex education, and other elements of the curriculum are objectionable to their faith.

Perhaps the most serious objection to large scale public education is the surrender of their children to professional educators – outsiders who have little understanding of humility, of earning one's bread with the sweat of one's brow. The Amish and Old Order Mennonites fear these outsiders will urge their children to emphasize their individual abilities, and this would necessarily lead them away from family, farm and faith. It is a risk the Plain community will not take.

An eager hand is raised during class in a one-room school. Plain children are very eager to learn, and try hard to please their teachers.

From the mid-1930s through the 1960s, Plain communities increasingly took control of their local schools. But not without some turmoil. Many Amish and Old Order Mennonite fathers were jailed for refusing to send their children to consolidated elementary schools, and many were prosecuted for refusing to send their children to high schools for education beyond the eighth grade. In most states, some compromise was reached, while in others, like Nebraska, the Amish left rather than send their children to school beyond eighth grade.

Finally, a 1972 ruling by the United States Supreme Court on a case involving an Amish family ended the controversy, and recognized the right of the Amish and other Plain groups to guide the education of their children based on their religious beliefs.

As part of the decision, Chief Justice Warren Burger wrote "Amish objection to formal education beyond the eighth grade is firmly grounded in central religious beliefs. They object to the high school and higher education generally because the values it teaches are in marked variance with Amish values and the Amish way of life. The high school tends to emphasize intellectual and scientific accomplishments, self-distinction, competitiveness, worldly success, and social life with other students. Amish society emphasizes informal learning-through-doing, a life of 'goodness,' rather than a life of intellect; wisdom, rather than technical knowledge; community welfare, rather than competition; and separation rather than integration with contemporary worldly society."

Today, most Plain communities operate their own one-room schools. They do so without any state or federal assistance. Their students are well prepared to become productive members of their community and church. By the time they reach fifth grade, both Rosanna and Rachel will be bilingual. Young Elam is already proficient in English. They speak German dialect at home, and are learning to speak, read and write English at school.

Two students, ready to leave for home, receive some final instructions and a word of encouragement from their teacher.

An Amish girl works studiously on her assignment while her teacher works with children in other grades. Students in one-room schools are seated in rows by grade.

Baseball games at recess time
are a favorite activity at one-
room schools. Many of the
best players are girls.

Rosanna and Rachel excitedly walk home. They know there will be a "house full", and they are eager to visit with their aunts. The evening chores will go quickly, and there will be fabric scraps to collect from the quilts, and baked treats to sample. They will be allowed to sew a few stitches on the quilt, and show their growing skill as well as contribute to the Sister's Day effort.

All the members of this wedding party are members of the Spring Garden Amish Mennonite Church.

RUMSPRINGA

David is in the midst of what the Amish call *rumspringa*, or the "running around" time of adolescence. Rumspringa is a transitional time between childhood and adulthood. It is a time for courtship, and a time when parents choose not to notice the high-spirited behavior of their children. For David it is a time of freedom and change. It is a time when Amish child-rearing practices, the goal of which is baptism and a commitment to the Plain way of life, is put to the test.

At his sixteenth birthday, David received his own harness, one of the traditional prerequisites to courting. He began to participate in Sunday evening sings. Sings are the main social activity for young, unmarried Plain people. Among the Amish the sings are held at the same home as the Sunday church service, usually in the barn, while Mennonite youth meet at local schools. At the sing the girls will sit on one side of the room and the boys on the other side facing them. Often young people from other church districts attend.

In some areas, sings may be rowdy and go far beyond what is allowed by the church. Several hundred young people may attend, and the occasion takes on the character of a barn dance. Country music and beer drinking may be a part of the evening that will go on until two or three o'clock the next morning. This kind of behavior is cause for great concern and more than a little embarrassment for the Plain parents.

Their harnesses and their driving horses, such as the horse being worked here, are a source of pride for young Amish men.

During rumspringa, Amish youngsters form informal groups called "crowds." The crowd a young Amish or Mennonite person chooses is a very serious matter. These cliques have distinct characters and range from relatively wild to conservative. The crowds are named according to their attitudes or local area. The Kirkwoods, named for their home area of Kirkwood, are a very conservative group. The Antiques are very liberal, and members are apt to have cars. Most members of the Groffies, the most liberal crowd of the past generation, owned cars and eventually left the Amish church. Other groups, like the Chickadees and the Cardinals, are groups of young friends who spend their time together much the way their parents and grandparents did when they were growing up.

Crowds spend much of their time socializing at parties they call "hops." There are volley ball hops, where a crowd will gather for

Two courting Amish couples enjoy a Sunday afternoon outing in a row boat on a quiet farm pond.

an afternoon of play, and supper hops where each of the girls in the crowd will bring a covered dish for all to share. "Hen hops" are pajama parties, and the girls try to keep the location a secret from the boys.

Elam and Sarah were very concerned when David fell in with a crowd known as the Cowboys. They knew that many members owned cars, and they suspected beer drinking. In the last year, David has outgrown his wildness, and settled down somewhat. Much to Elam and Sarah's relief, David has become part of a more conservative "all buggy" crowd. They still have concerns though: the young men have begun to take hunting trips in the Pennsylvania mountains. These trips require hiring an "English" driver and Sarah worries that they may become too worldly. She was reassured when David brought home a buck.

Most Amish youth pass from running around to dating, and then to going steady. David has probably found a "steady" and that has contributed to his better behavior. In most cases, going steady will lead to marriage.

Courtship among the Amish and Old Order Mennonites was traditionally conducted almost secretly. Young men would meet their steady at the end of the lane, or arrive at their house long after her parents had gone to bed. No longer secret, courtship is still a very private matter. Often friends and family members will not know about a couple's marriage plans until it is announced at church.

Before young Plain couples can marry, they must be baptized, signifying their commitment to the church and the Plain way of life. There are many distinctive wedding customs that vary from settlement to settlement. Among the Amish and Old Order Mennonites weddings are held on Tuesdays or Thursdays. Among the Lancaster County Plain people, weddings are almost always held in November or December. In other settlements, weddings may be held at any time.

Weddings are both a serious and a festive occasion. Marriage is an important passage into adult life for Plain people. It is a serious commitment between two people who must work together to provide for themselves and the family that will follow. This is reflected in the church service.

Weddings are also celebrations. They are important social occasions in the Plain community. Many Amish shops and businesses close for a day, or alter their work schedules, often during November and December, to accommodate attendance at weddings. Weddings are festive occasions that bring families and friends together, often from far-away locations, for a day of singing, feasting and gift-giving honoring the newly-married couple. They are also a celebration of the continuation of the Plain way of life.

Top: a deep winter snow is all that is needed to bring out the horse and sleigh for a delightful ride along country roads or through the fields.

Young Plain people often enjoy visiting the Ephrata Cloisters, a restored monastery founded in 1735 by German dissenters calling themselves the Society of the Solitary. It is now operated as an historic site by the State of Pennsylvania.

An Amish buggy travels down a quiet farm road with the autumn foliage of the Conewango Valley as a colorful backdrop.

CHAPTER FOUR
WORK

The Plain People practice
their ethic of hard work as
farmers, craftsmen and
businessmen

~

A steel-wheeled tractor is
defined by a blazing setting
sun. Tractors fitted with steel
wheels are permitted in the
fields by some Mennonite
groups. The steel wheels
restrict use of the tractor to
the fields by making it
unusable for transportation
on paved roads.

A pair of fancy draft horses about to enter the ring at winter auction. As a rule, work horses are sold in pairs.

IT IS A COLD January morning. The sky is clear, and the sun bright. A team of horses moves methodically across the field, first to the east, and then returning to the west. They are large draft animals bred for work. As they plod through the field, their heavy breath is visible as it condenses in the sharp chill of the morning. Levi Stoltzfus is spreading manure over his fields, as his father did before him. For Levi, and other Amish and Old Order Mennonite farmers in Lancaster County, tilling the soil is more than just a job. It is a way of life, a tradition, and a link in the chain that connects their faith with the past and future.

A typical day for Levi and the other Plain farmers in Lancaster County begins before dawn. Before breakfast the livestock will be tended, dairy cows milked, manure pits shoveled out, and hay brought down from the loft. Silage will be shoveled down from the silo and hay fed to the horses, heifers and mules. All the work is done by hand. There are few machines and often no electricity on these farms.

Farming is a family activity, and all but the youngest children join in the chores. Sleeping late is almost unheard of. Young men often work alongside their fathers and carry much of the burden of running the farm. Younger boys assist their fathers and brothers and learn the skills necessary to be a good farmer. Levi's oldest son Aaron, aged eighteen, helps farm full time and will someday purchase the family farm from his father. Aaron's younger brother, Ben, is working as a "hired boy" on the dairy farm of a neighbor and fellow church member to learn more about the dairy business, as well as to earn a modest income.

The children perform a variety of chores both in the kitchen and the barn. The children begin to learn the work ethic and responsibility needed to be successful farmers by feeding the ducks and chickens, always under the watchful eyes of older siblings. Finding eggs and taking care of small livestock are the work of the younger children, along with helping their older brothers and sisters. On dairy farms, it is usually left to the girls to clean up the barn after milking. Stripping and grading tobacco is family work, and all help under the supervision of an adult. By grading the tobacco before sale the Amish farmer earns more per pound. Small children, until they are five, stay in the kitchen or barn under the watchful eye of parents.

Children often turn their chores into games. Singing is a popular activity, and children often sing while they work. Levi's children can often be heard singing songs such as *"Uns zu ermahnen durch dein Wort."*

It is Levi's hope that his sons will continue to farm. He will do all he can to ensure this by helping them acquire land. It is unusual for farms to be sold outside the family. Frequently, the oldest son will buy his father's farm, the father then retiring to the "grossdawdy" house on the same farm. If the farm does not go to a son, it may go to a son-in-law or other relative.

Levi is Amish, a member of a church that is known as one of the more conservative districts. While they reject the use of tractors in the fields, the use of gasoline-powered motors to operate devices like hay balers and corn binders is allowed – as long as they are

A Plain farmer tills the land in preparation for spring planting. His plow is drawn through the soil by a six-horse team.

pulled by a team of horses. Most Old Order Mennonites and Amish have tractors in the barn, but not for use in the fields. Tractor power for operating feed grinders, wheat threshers and blowing silage into silos is allowed by the church, and necessary. Electricity is forbidden among the Amish, although among many Old Order Mennonites it is permissible.

On a farm, the work is never finished, but because it is January the pace of life for Levi and his wife Anna is somewhat slower. December and January are important months for slaughtering meat animals, preparing tobacco for market, and visiting friends and relatives, both close by and far away. Harnesses are mended in February, and plowing is under way by March. These are important months for farm sales of everything from machinery and animals to land and buildings.

Riding the mules or sitting high atop the hay makes bringing in the hay a working "hay ride" for these boys near Quarryville, Pennsylvania. Plain kids take every opportunity to turn their chores into fun.

Potatoes are planted in April, and throughout the warm weather the cycle of planting and tending crops is followed. Corn is planted in April, tobacco in May. Every farm has a large garden. Alfalfa and hay are first cut in June. Cultivation continues until September and October when the harvest begins. Corn, potatoes, tobacco and alfalfa all must be harvested, and this work continues into November. November and December are also months traditionally set aside for weddings.

TAKING A CROP TO MARKET

January is important in Pennsylvania because it is the time when tobacco is brought to market. Tobacco is a traditional cash crop for many Amish and Old Order Mennonite farmers in the Lancaster area. It "pays the feed bill" over the winter when many farmers are between crops, and times are lean.

Levi doesn't grow tobacco. The market three years ago took a dramatic and unexpected downward turn. The experience left Levi and many of his neighbors unwilling to plant tobacco again. It is a traditional cash crop, but other things such as truck farming, especially melons, are almost as valuable, and the market much more reliable. Both tobacco and truck farming are labor intensive and will keep the whole family busy in the fields. It was an easy exchange.

The Amish and Old Order Mennonites of Lancaster County may grow tobacco or not, depending on what suits their farm and family. For the Amish in Indiana and Ohio, growing tobacco is forbidden. It is not a proper activity. The morality of growing tobacco is a frequent topic in the Amish monthly *Family Life*. It is frequently a subject of discussion when Amish from different settlements gather. For instance, when older Amish meet in Florida during the winter, tobacco will often be discussed, along with the price of draft animals and crops.

While Levi doesn't grow tobacco, he and his oldest son Aaron will attend the auction. They will also help Levi's brother Ike haul his crop there. Once it is delivered they will stay to meet with other farmers, exchange stories and catch up on the news of the local community.

The tobacco barn in Paradise, Lancaster County, is filled with long rows of pallet after pallet of tobacco. Each pallet has bales of the leaf stacked according to grade. Maryland grade brings the highest price and is used for cigarettes. Pennsylvania grade sells for less and is used for cigars, chewing tobacco and snuff.

The growers gather early, and as their tobacco is unloaded and stacked they gather in the coffee shop, or outside where the horses

Harrowing further breaks up the soil after plowing as the land is prepared for spring planting. Plain farmers devote much time and attention to their soil throughout the year.

Cultivating new corn (facing page) is grueling but necessary work to keep the young corn plants ahead of the weeds. It is a chore with which the whole family will help.

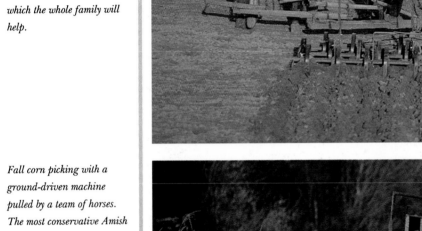

Fall corn picking with a ground-driven machine pulled by a team of horses. The most conservative Amish still harvest corn completely by hand.

Overleaf: an Amish farmer works his fields. As the young corn grows larger, hand cultivating gives way to a horse drawn sulky cultivator.

Plowing with a walk-behind plow is backbreaking work for this Mennonite farmer. This plowing technique is still in use only among the most conservative.

A young girl is undaunted by the attention of the large draft animals surrounding her.

A team of mules pulls the last wagon load of summer hay at the end of a hard day in the fields.

A carpet of leaves is an ideal playground for an Amish girl and her puppy.

and carriages are tethered. The conversation concerns crop prices and local events. How much a 54-acre farm near Strasburg was sold for last week, whose sons were married during this season, and other local events are common topics.

There are many men in Plain dress. At first glance to an "English" outsider they all look uniform. Only later does it become apparent that there are several distinct groups. The Amish men are well represented and recognizable by their beards, round crowned hats with wide brims, and suspenders. There are also many Old Order Mennonites, distinguished by their black fedora-style hats. Some are clean shaven. Even the sounds of this sale are distinctive. The predominant language among the growers is German dialect. Only the "English" farmers, those wearing blue denim overalls and down vests are speaking English in their conversations.

Finally, all the buyers have arrived and the sale is ready to proceed. The seven buyers line up on one side of the row of pallets loaded with tobacco, with the auctioneer and staff on the other side. The auctioneer has come to Paradise from the South to conduct the auction. With a deep voice and North Carolina accent, the auctioneer begins his song at the first pallet, and his assistant calls out "1-32" ($1.32 a pound) to start the bidding.

Moments after the bidding starts, the growers are astounded. Within seconds, the price has soared to $1.74, an historic high price.

The auction is halted and the buyers scurry for telephones to seek instructions. The auction resumes and, before the third pallet is sold, several buyers ask for yet another delay. The sale ultimately resumes and a floor price of $1.72 for Maryland tobacco is established.

The Plain growers' reaction reflects their humility. There is little outward celebration or emotion. But it is clear, from the initial looks of surprise and the ripple of murmured German dialect, to the subsequent looks of satisfaction, that there are many pleased farmers whose labor has been very well rewarded today. Levi and Aaron are pleased for Ike and the other growers, but know all too well the other extreme.

The first breath of spring brings seagulls far inland through the Susquehanna River Valley into Lancaster County to feast on the worms and grubs in the freshly turned soil.

Chores and smiles. Top: feeding calves is typical work for young boys.

Right: some of the string beans will be used on the dinner table, the remainder will be canned for winter use.

Overleaf: a young boy scurries through the early morning haze to avoid being late for school.

Not all Plain people are farmers. While farming is at the core of all Amish, Old Order Mennonite and Hutterite settlements, many make their living using other skills and practicing other occupations.

The carriage shop operated by Abner Lapp in Intercourse is an interesting example of the artisan's skill and craftsmanship that has become a mainstay of Plain communities. Lapp's carriage shop was one of the first Amish shops to build and repair carriages. Before the automobile, the Amish community relied on the carriage and wagon shops operated by their non-Amish neighbors. As the automobile steadily replaced the carriage among the non-Amish, Lapp's was the first Amish business in Lancaster County established to meet the continuing need of the Plain community for carriage work. Lapp's began by building and repairing the traditional buggies and carriages favored by the Amish and many Old Order Mennonites. Over the last generation, since Abner took over the shop from his father, it has become increasingly well known for its restoration work on classic and antique carriages and wagons.

Today, Abner Lapp and his crew spend their days restoring Victorian carriages from all over the United States and Europe to their original beauty. There is a long waiting list for their skill and craftsmanship. A look in the shop might reveal a brougham, surrey or cabriolet in various stages of repair or restoration. These are carriages that carried Presidents and Kings.

One shop worker specializes in interiors, and is equally skilled at leather or cloth upholstery. The wheelwright rebuilds wheel assemblies, replacing spokes with new ones turned to order. Often new wheels will be built to match old. Body repair and refinishing requires woodworking and metal skills. Carriages are not just painted, they require the right finish. Every aspect of coach work is carried out at Lapp's.

Abner and his co-workers are all Amish. They all live within a short distance of the shop, most close enough to return home for lunch. They do not own cars and rely on buggies as their primary transportation. They do all of their work with tools powered by hand or air, as Abner and his craftsmen are prohibited from using electric-powered tools. They are permitted to use pneumatic tools, powered by forced air, driven by a diesel powered compressor. Some Amish craftsmen use tools powered by hydraulic power or battery. Craftsmen like Abner Lapp continue to prove that the source of power will never be as important as the artisan using the tool.

Woodworking is a craft that has always been practiced by Plain people, and their work is highly sought after because of its beauty and artistry.

Ben Shirk is typical of many woodworkers. He works in a small

Hand-made cane rocking chairs are typical of the workmanship and beauty of the woodworking practiced by many Plain people in small, home workshops.

The blacksmith shop is an important part of every horse-and-buggy community. This blacksmith's shop is located in Kidron, Ohio.

Snowfall covers two wagons and a sleigh being offered for sale outside an antiques shop near Intercourse, Pennsylvania.

shop next to the barn on his farm. Ben learned woodworking as a young boy, and was employed by a Plain woodworker before he married. After marriage, Ben turned to farming full time, but continued wood working as a secondary occupation, selling his cabinet work privately, or to shop owners. When his eldest son became old enough to take over operation of the farm, Ben returned to woodworking full time. He is often assisted by one of his grandchildren as he sands, cuts, glues and pegs roll top desks, bookshelves, cabinets and bed headboards. All of Ben's power tools are driven by air or hydraulic power, and he still uses more hand tools than other non-Plain woodworkers.

Ben is a Mennonite and a member of the Wenger church. For

A child shyly peers from inside the family buggy on a farm near Ethridge, Tennessee.

members of the Wenger Mennonite church electricity is optional. Many younger members have accepted electricity, while many older members, like Ben, have continued to follow the old practice. "Why, I wouldn't know how to work it," Ben, with a wry smile, answered a recent visitor's question about electricity. Wengers also allow the use of tractors, and other power equipment in the fields – provided that the machines are equipped with steel wheels to ensure they will not be used on the highway.

There are many larger woodworking and cabinet work businesses operated by Plain people. They range from other small family enterprises to those that resemble small factories. Family businesses that grow rely on other family members, cousins, nephews as well as other church members for their employees. Larger businesses still prefer to hire other Plain people, often from the owner's congregation and community. Frequently, there will be a position

After eighteen years of hard work in the fields, "Sparky," a large Morgan stallion, enjoys his retirement and new status as the family pet.

for at least one "English" person as the designated driver to provide transportation as needed.

Ben is 73 years old, and he works in his shop every day except Sunday. He enjoys his work, and his craftsmanship is enjoyed by many eager customers. A child's spiral bound copy book serves as his order book. "I'm not looking for new business," says Ben. "I need to live to be a hundred to finish all that's written down here."

BUSINESS

As many Plain settlements have grown, there has been an increase in the demand for land. The supply of good, arable land has been

A steam-powered tractor manufactured in the 1920s is still at work providing belt power for a threshing crew on a Plain farm near Kinzer, Pennsylvania.

taken by succeeding generations of farmers. As the arable land came under cultivation, the price began to increase with demand. The lack of good land at reasonable prices in larger Plain settlements has forced many to find other ways to earn a living.

Some have actively turned to commerce. Applying the same ethic of hard work to the market place as to farming, many Plain people operate successful businesses. Plain people can be found engaged in businesses as diverse as foundries, health food distributors, printing shops, carpentry and building trades, and retail shops catering to tourists in towns like Berlin, in Holmes County, Ohio.

Some businesses have been forced on the Plain community. The importance of battery power to the Amish has given rise to an Amish-owned business producing the Pequea battery. The prohibition against electricity has given rise to an active industry in refitting appliances, such as washing machines, from electric power to gasoline.

An Amish farmer, a member of the conservative Nebraska group, cuts hay with a horse-drawn, ground-powered cutter near Belleville, Pennsylvania.

Overleaf: sunset lights up the horizon behind a large Amish farmhouse, as dark, brooding clouds above offer some hope for rain.

A large Belgian draft horse stands harnessed and ready for work in the fields. Belgians are a popular breed of draft animal because of their endurance and strength.

Similarly, many businesses that manufacture and repair horse drawn farm machinery are owned and operated by Amish and Old Order Mennonites. One inventive Amishman developed a hay turner that flips hay upside down to allow it to dry faster while in the field. Ironically, the hay turner is in highest demand for use with tractors, and can be found on farms all across America.

Recently, a farmer established a small foundry business to manufacture parts for the steam engine used to sterilize his tobacco fields. The "English" company that had manufactured the needed parts went out of business. This Amish farmer bought the molds and set up his own foundry, now an ongoing business.

In many retail shops run by Amish and Old Order Mennonites certain characteristics stand out. In Miller's Health Foods store, or Zook's Dry Goods in Lancaster County, the overhead light is supplied by gas burning fixtures. The dry goods stores offer a far larger selection of bolt fabric and other sewing supplies than do most specialty sewing shops located in suburban malls. Televisions, electrical appliances, tapes and records are among the things that will not be found in shops owned by Plain people.

Shocks of wheat drying in the field are arranged in orderly rows. The absence of a tangle of telephone and electrical lines on the Plain farm and in the surrounding countryside is a sure sign that all the farms in this area are Amish.

An aerial view of a Lancaster County Amish farm reveals the subtle and graceful pattern of freshly cut hay in the field.

THE MARKETPLACE

Taking farm products to market has evolved into a thriving and profitable business for many. From the Reading Terminal Market in the heart of downtown Philadelphia, to the historic Central Market in the city of Lancaster, to the Belleville Market in the most conservative Amish community in rural Pennsylvania, Amish and Old Order Mennonites can be found selling the produce of their farms, and the handiwork of their crafts.

Many, like the Stoltzfus family, have combined farming with marketing, and take their own produce to market two or three days a week.

The Stoltzfus family travels every Thursday, Friday and Saturday from their farm in Lancaster County to a nearby farmers' market to sell their meats and produce. They also sell the products of other local farms and food producers. In the summer, Anna's garden produces corn, tomatoes, and many other vegetables. Eggs from a neighboring farm, meats from local growers, and seasonal fruits like apples are an important part of their market.

In the winter there is less home-grown produce to sell, and emphasis shifts to locally-produced meats and baked goods. Anna will still offer produce delivered by an "English" driver with a truck because she does not want to disappoint her customers. "But it's not as good, not as good as what we grow here." There is always space on the shelf for small wooden animals cut by a local woodworker, or a quilt offered for sale by a neighbor.

It requires tremendous work on Thursday, Friday and Saturday, involving the whole family, to do both the farm chores and sell at the market. The days are long and difficult, but it has been a very successful arrangement, providing the Stoltzfus' with a stable income from a profitable business. More importantly, it is a business that does not take them away from farm life, or challenge their commitment to their faith.

Over the years, some Plain people have become full time merchants at farmers' markets. They buy products from a variety of purveyors, including their neighbors, and sell to customers who frequent the market. They offer fresh meats, vegetables, fruits and eggs. Some specialize in baked goods, while other operate stands where fresh soft pretzels are rolled and baked.

An example of how large this market activity can grow is the Esh family egg business. This has grown up from its origin as a family-based business, and now must employ people from outside the family, including many non-Plain people. The Esh family sells eggs retail and wholesale from their facility located across the road from the family home in Lancaster County. The family also sells eggs and dairy products at markets in nearby Hatville and Booth's Corner.

Horse and buggies travel a country road that has become a ribbon of gold in the setting sun.

Little girls accompany their father to market.
A Mennonite girl watches over her family's stand.
Selling quilts at auction has become an important source of additional income for many Plain families.

An Amish housewife, a member of the "yellow top" group, tends her market stand at the Belleville farmers' market. The Belleville area is known as the Big Valley, and is home to a number of different Amish groups often distinguished by the color of their buggy tops.

Amish boys try their hand at hawking horseshoes and homemade wreaths at the end of a farm lane to capitalize on the ever-growing Lancaster County tourist industry.

An outdoor stand features quilts. The quilts may be sewn by the Amish housewife tending the stand, or by family members, friends or neighbors. Quilting has always been a tradition among Plain women, and now it is a source of extra money for the household as well.

*Farmers, many of them
Plain, line up to offer their
produce for sale at a local
auction. Once sold, the
produce is distributed to
markets and stores for retail
sale.*

*Large pumpkins are ready
for sale at the market.*

On Thursdays, Fridays and Saturdays, David Esh's egg stand is one of the most prominent and successful businesses located in the historic Reading Terminal Market in the heart of Philadelphia.

Taking products to market is an easy task for all when the market is nearby. As members of Plain faiths that do not permit automobiles reach out to meet the demand in markets outside the immediate area, other arrangements must be made. Often drivers must be hired to take the merchants and their goods to markets too far away for horse and carriage. In Lancaster County, a small service industry has grown up around the need for Amish and other Plain merchants to reach markets that seem to get farther and farther away. Some enterprising Lancaster Plain people have established markets as far away as suburban Washington, DC. "Amish taxi drivers" provide a valuable service that allows many merchants to expand their businesses into new areas. At the close of business at many markets in southeastern Pennsylvania, like the Reading Terminal Market, Plain people can be seen loading their remaining goods, and then boarding vans belonging to "English" drivers for the long ride home.

FARMS AND LAND

An Amish scarecrow at work guarding an early spring garden. Scarecrows are not commonly found in Amish gardens. This scarecrow's work schedule, like his clothing, is typically Amish. After a long week in the garden, he is taken out of the ground on Sunday, reappearing early Monday morning.

Farming has been the preferred occupation of the Amish, Hutterites and Old Order Mennonites for generations. In some areas farm land has become scarce and other occupations have been pursued. But among the Plain people birth rates are high, and there are always more sons than farms.

While the success of non-farming occupations is appreciated, farming still holds a special place for the Plain people. The lack of arable land at reasonable, or even exorbitant, prices in the Lancaster County area, has led Noah Martin to buy two farms in Iowa, in an area that has not been settled by Plain people.

Noah Martin is a dairy farmer. He has a herd of 48 dairy cows on a 40-acre farm. His farm is half of the farm his father worked. Noah bought his acreage from his father, and went into dairy farming because it seemed the best way to earn a living on his smaller farm. His brother Amos farms the other half of the original acreage. Their father and mother still help out, and have moved to the "grossdawdy" house attached to the main house where Amos and his family now live.

A big red barn stands out against the rolling hills of the Conewango Valley in western New York. This area was first settled in the 1940s by conservative Amish families from Ohio.

If all goes well, Noah's two oldest sons and their families will move to Iowa. They will be followed by other Old Order Mennonite families from their area as word spreads of land available at reasonable prices. Friends and relatives will learn about the farms and the planned move from Noah and his family.

A note about the move may appear in *The Budget*, or *Die Botschaft*, newspapers devoted to open letters written by Plain people from all over North America. They are an important source of information about people and conditions in other settlements. Other Plain people across North America will read that the sons of Noah Martin have moved to Iowa. Others, especially in Noah's church district, will consider the area as a place for their sons to farm and continue their way of life. While Noah's sons will lead the way, once it is published in *The Budget*, the way will be clear for others to follow.

It will be difficult at first to establish a new farm in an unfamiliar area. The soil will need to be built up, housekeeping established, and eventually a school and meeting house for worship will be built. It will also be lonely compared to the activity and hubbub of the larger settlements, such as Berlin, in Holmes County, Ohio, or Intercourse, in Lancaster County, Pennsylvania. But soon others will follow. A church district will be established and worship services will be held. Communion will be offered once each year. The yearly cycle of Plain Life will continue.

FARMING 10,000 ACRES

Among the Hutterites, land is not a problem. Its what to do with all of it, and how to make it productive. The majority of Hutterite colonies, called *Bruderhofs*, are located in the Great Plains states of South Dakota and Montana, and the Provinces of Manitoba, Saskatchewan and Alberta. This is called the "Big Sky Country" of high snow capped mountains, a seemingly never-ending blue sky, and an unreachable horizon.

Nestled in to the sheltered valleys, far off the highway, are Hutterite settlements with names like Downey Lake, Pincher Creek, and Jasper Springs. From these settlements, Hutterite men perform much the same work as any other modern American cowboy, although they hardly fit the popular image of the American West, dressed as they are in traditional black pants, print shirts and suspenders.

This Amish farmhouse has had several additions built on to it to accommodate succeeding generations.

Overleaf: a young boy tends to the family dairy herd, driving the cows into the meadow after milking.

128

The oldest house is the red one (facing page top), with other houses being added over the years. Each addition is a separate house. The grandparents moved from the red house to the smaller white house that is now known as the "grossdawdy" house.

Facing page bottom: a large Amish dairy farm is surrounded by cornfields with other farms in the background. These farms are located near Georgetown, Pennsylvania.

Hutterite colonies are self-contained communal villages that must engage in a variety of agricultural activities just to sustain themselves. Most colonies work thousands of acres of land, combining farming of crops such as wheat and barley with livestock like beef and sheep, while also maintaining their own gardens. Colonies also produce a variety of other products. They grow their own grapes for wine, and tend beehives to produce honey.

Every colony has a "householder" or "boss" who is the business manager of the colony. He is responsible for the economic well-being of the colony, and all its financial dealings. But it is the "farm boss" or "field boss" who is responsible for the effective and efficient operation of the farm and all its related activities. Those responsible for the cattle, sheep, chickens and ducks, as well as the mechanic who maintains the machinery, and the carpenter, all come under the direction of the farm boss.

Fortunately, there are no prohibitions against farm machinery that increases communal productivity among the Hutterites. Many Bruderhofs have over 10,000 acres of land, much of it stubborn and hard to work. Most Bruderhofs have the latest in equipment, including bulldozers, tractors and combines. The colony shop is capable of making numerous tools and implements, many of them quite sophisticated.

Many conservative Amish continue to milk cows by hand and place the milk in cans at the end of farm lanes to be picked up by the dairy. The milk is used only for cheese because the Amish farmers have refused to use mechanized refrigerated bulk tanks now required for table quality milk.

On most dairy farms calves are weaned early and not allowed to suckle, to conserve the valuable milk of the mother cow. The important work of the care and feeding of calves belongs to the children.

A young girl attends milking machines in the dairy barn of her family's farm near New Holland, Pennsylvania. Her family belongs to the Beachy Amish Mennonite group that left the Amish Church and has since accepted many forms of technology, including milking machines and tractors for use in the fields.

Above right: a Plain farmer who has held the line on technology and uses a mechanical picker pulled by teams of horses to pick corn on his farm.

Right: the hard labor of spearing tobacco in the field is turned into an occasion for these girls to visit.

A typical Bruderhof of 10,000 acres will raise wheat, barley and hay on its arable land. Much of the hay will be used as feed for its livestock. The less arable land will be used for grazing cattle. Livestock might include a herd of 500 or more cattle and a dairy herd of 50 cows. Other livestock includes approximately 1000 lambs raised each year as a source of meat and wool for market, as well as lamb for the Bruderhof's table. Hogs are raised year round. Chickens, ducks and geese might also be raised, both for the table and the market place. In some areas potatoes are an important cash crop.

While the men work the farm and handle the livestock, the women of the Bruderhof help with the garden. Among the Hutterites "the garden" is no mere back yard plot. An efficient Bruderhof will have a large and varied truck garden to produce vegetables for its own use. It takes many hands to tend so large a garden, and the distinctive dark blue scarfs with white polka dots worn by the women as they go about their work stand out against the green tops of the carrots, parsnips and turnips that are a part of most gardens.

The scale of farming on the Bruderhof is impressive. According to a recent visitor, "If they raise one chicken, they will raise 10,000 chickens. If they're going to have ducks, they will raise 10,000 ducks."

While the Hutterites are known for their agricultural efficiency and success, it is still a struggle to overcome the elements of this rugged country. In spite of the elements, however, many of the Hutterite colonies have become important commercial growers of poultry and vegetables in their region, selling directly to supermarket chains and food packers.

When they reach the age of fifteen young men are assigned jobs. They are often given the jobs that are well suited to their youth, like operating bulldozers, and riding the range. Young women begin to work closely with the adult women in the kitchen, laundry and garden. The young workers experience a variety of jobs on the Bruderhof and serve as apprentices.

Above left: the color and aroma of a cornucopia of fresh vegetables fills the stands of the Green Dragon Market near Ephrata, Pennsylvania.

Left: an Amish daughter cleans beets from the family garden. These beets will all find their way to the family table. Some will be cooked or pickled immediately, while the rest will be canned and preserved for use over the winter.

Overleaf: this "Prairie Castle" serves the Hutterite colonies located near Maple Creek, Saskatchewan.

CHAPTER FIVE

THE AMISH, HUTTERITES AND OLD ORDER MENNONITES TODAY

Contemporary Plain People,

living in successful

communities that are growing

~

"Trick or treating" is a rare Halloween game for these four Amish lasses disguised in homemade masks. The practice is frowned upon in most Amish church districts.

A young lad guides his team through the fields as they disk the soil. Disking is an important part of the spring preparations for planting.

F ROM THEIR FIRST settlements in the 17th and 18th centuries, the Plain People have grown in number, and spread geographically, establishing new settlements. Their growth in numbers has been driven by large families rather than converts. Their geographic spread has been driven by their agricultural lifestyle, and their need to acquire more farm land to support their growing numbers.

Amish, Old Order Mennonites and Hutterites do not report population statistics. The size and growth of their populations can only be estimated, and can best be estimated from the number of congregations that exist.

A M I S H

There are currently 660 church districts or congregations spread throughout twenty states and the Province of Ontario. These congregations represent 175 settlements or communities. The size of communities range from a single church district, which is usually comprised of about nine families, to the largest community of 111 church districts, located in Ohio. The Amish population is estimated to be 120,000 men, women and children.

The Amish population, because of its high birth rate, nearly doubles every twenty years. The best illustration of the spread of the Amish population is that of the 175 communities that exist today, 70 per cent were established since 1960. The largest concentration of Amish population continues to be found in the larger, older settlements. Approximately 70 per cent of the Amish population live in these older, established communities in Indiana, Ohio and Pennsylvania.

Lancaster County, Pennsylvania is the oldest Amish settlement, founded in 1760, and today has the densest concentration of Amish population. It has 77 church districts. The largest settlement is centered in Holmes County, Ohio and has 111 church districts. Next in size of population is the LaGrange-Elkhart County settlement in Indiana with 54 church districts.

Settlements in Michigan and New York have experienced rapid growth. The number of settlements in Michigan grew from six in the mid-1970s, to eighteen by 1985. New York's number of Amish settlements during the same time span rose from two to twelve.

The Amish have recently settled in far off states where there have never been Amish before. Settlements have been established in Arkansas, Montana and Texas. Not all settlements are successful.

Two young Mennonite girls hand pick potatoes. Harvesting potatoes requires long days of labor by the whole family, and often friends and relatives are enlisted to help turn the chore into a game.

Some newly-established settlements never realise the critical mass of families needed to sustain the Plain way of life, or they find that the land will not support them. The settlers are forced to disperse to other settlements in search of better land and a stable community. It remains to be seen if these new settlements will be able to establish themselves both economically and spiritually.

The most conservative of the Amish are the Swartzentruber Amish of Ohio, and the Nebraska Amish of Pennsylvania, called Nebraska because an important Bishop in the formation of their church district came to the district from Nebraska. More liberal

districts, at least in terms of farming technology, are found in Kalona, Iowa, and Haven, Kansas, where tractors are often used in the field.

The Amish have had several major schisms in their history, and those factions that have left the church are not counted here as Amish. In 1910 a group left the Amish in a dispute over shunning, and the use of new technologies that were being introduced – electricity, cars and telephones. The group that broke away in 1910 became known as the Beachy Amish Mennonites. They maintain many Plain customs, such as dress, but do not follow the Amish prohibitions against technology. Today there about 7,000 adult members of this group.

Dressed for church, the children are ready to take off in the family buggy. Amish children are remarkably well behaved in church, where services typically last up to four hours.

The weekly shopping trip to the local farmers' market (above left) is a treat for the children and a welcome break from the routine of the farm for their mothers.

The Amish of Indiana are well known for their very large flower gardens (above). The gardens are not only a tradition, but a means of self expression for many Indiana Amish housewives.

Two sisters return an errant goat to its pen. Taking care of the small animals is a part of every child's chores on farms among the Plain people.

Above left: grades one through eight hard at work on their assignments in this one-room school, while their teacher reviews the work of individual students.

Above: a young girl grimaces as one of her calves is dehorned. She and her brother have raised the calves and are responsible for their care.

This auction near Gordonville, Pennsylvania is well attended by Plain people. Auctions and sales serve as social events as well as a source of livestock.

A wagon ride goes with the evening chores for these two sisters.

Left: a Mennonite girl pauses while feeding the ducks and chickens to cradle a tiny duckling.

Mennonite families are often large, and it is not unusual for families to have ten or more children. Right: the names of fourteen siblings have been written in concrete at their farm.

Far right: a wagonfull of Mennonite farm girls giggle shyly at the prospect of being photographed.

Overleaf: on a clear, crisp winter morning Plain men crowd around a team of work horses ready for auction.

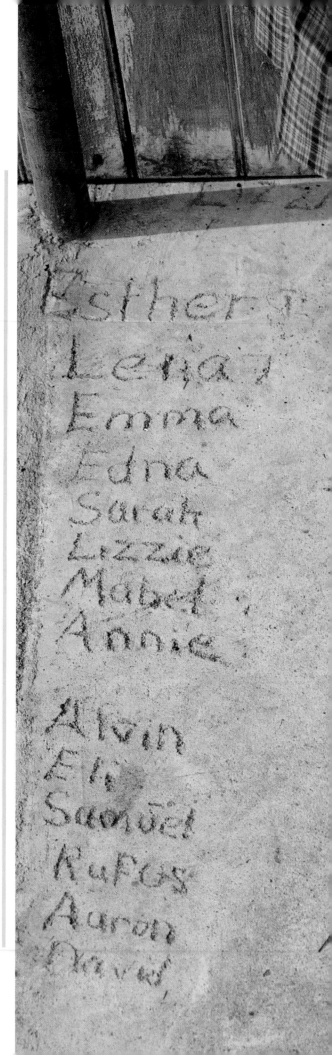

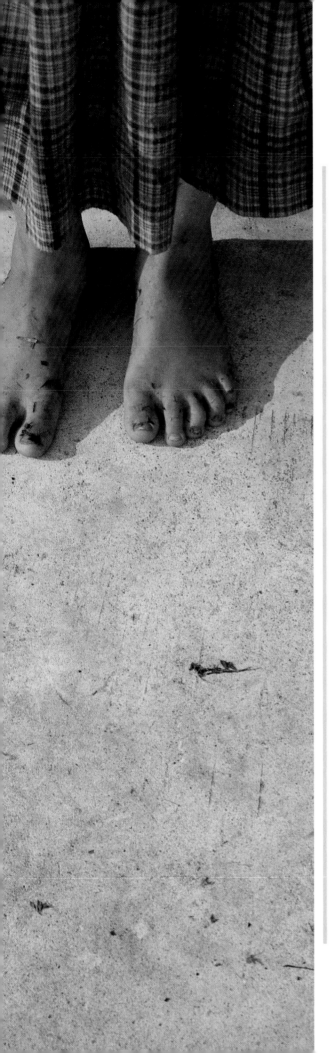

A large group calling themselves the New Order Amish broke away in 1966. Again, the reasons included the use of technology, and the disputed items included the deep freeze, combines, and electric generators. Each of these items, as well as others, had been slowly becoming a feature of many Amish farms. When the decision was made to "hold the line" on these worldly devices and have them "put away," many church members balked. Those who chose to leave also adopted the use of the tractor in the field, as well as electricity. This caused great dissension in some settlements. Some church districts in Lancaster went so far as to offer an "open door" policy that allowed families to leave without being shunned, in order to put the matter behind them. The New Order Amish soon splintered into several other groups over issues such as growing tobacco. They continue in most cases to dress Plain, but have abandoned the horse and carriage in favor of the automobile. There are several thousand adult members of these groups today.

OLD ORDER MENNONITES

The use of the term Old Order is a catch-all to describe the various groups of Mennonites that have withdrawn from the mainstream Mennonite Conferences to pursue a stricter, more conservative life

style. The first major divisions occurred in the mid-19th century. Since then there have been subsequent divisions, further splintering these groups. The essence of Old Order Mennonite practice is local and personal rather than bureaucratic, and it is of little consequence to the various congregations that they are not part of a large national conference.

THE GROFFDALE CONFERENCE

The Groffdale Conference Mennonite Church, known as the Wenger Mennonites, are the largest group of Old Order Mennonites. The Groffdale church was formed in 1893 through a division in the main Mennonite conference in Lancaster County, Pennsylvania. There is a wide variation in practices among Wenger members today. Among non-ordained members, the use of electricity and the telephone is allowed, although many choose not to accept these worldly technologies. There are also some Wengers who have outdoor toilets, reject the use of propane gas, and continue to use hand pumps in the kitchen. The Wenger church permits tractors, but they must be fitted with steel wheels.

Just as the Wenger faction left the Lancaster Mennonite conference because they felt it was becoming too liberal, a group of thirty-five families left the Wenger church to adopt more conservative practices. The Reidenbach Mennonite Church is also known as the "Thirty-fivers" for the original families broke away in 1946. The Reidenbachers reject electricity, telephones, and tractors for field work. There are four Reidenbach church districts.

The Old Order tendency toward divisions came full circle in 1990. A group of families left the Reidenbach church and "returned home," rejoining the Wenger Church.

The Wenger group has been the most aggressive of Lancaster County Plain groups to migrate out of the county. As farm land in Lancaster County has become more and more expensive, tourism based on the Plain community more intrusive, and the county's character becoming more suburban, many members of the Wenger group found it more difficult to live the Mennonite life they desired. In 1974, the first Wenger families moved to Yates County in New York. By 1989, Yates County supported 140 families, seven one-room schools, two meeting houses and 120 Wenger farms.

The Wenger immigration to Yates County revitalized a farming

Dressed for church, young Amish women stroll down the road. They wear traditional white Swiss organdy aprons over their black dresses. Although their cut and style may vary, organdy aprons are a part of the Sunday wardrobe of the women of every Amish settlement.

A deer adopted as a fawn from the wild and raised by this Amish family remains a favorite family pet.

Walking down a farm lane, little girls dressed for church pause to turn and wave.

community that had fallen on hard times. Wengers control over twenty per cent of all farms in the county, and are still buying. While the land is not as rich as Lancaster, the climate is good, and it is an agricultural community that is becoming stronger.

In Yates County, the Old Order Mennonites can realize their desire to farm the land, and to watch their sons grow up to farm. Arable land here can be purchased for about $700 an acre. In Lancaster County, farms have recently sold for between $5500 and $7000 per acre. And they need not worry about encroaching suburbs, or tour buses crowding their carriages on the highway.

OTHER OLD ORDER MENNONITES

The first major split from the mainstream Mennonite conferences resulted in the creation of several groups that remain among the most conservative of all Plain groups. The split took place in Lancaster County, Pennsylvania in 1845, when a group of conservative families left the Lancaster Conference of the Mennonite Church. This group became known as the Pike Mennonites.

The Pike group has divided into several other fellowships since then. Today, the groups that descended from the Pike group, such as the Stauffer fellowship and Noah Hoover group, are among the most conservative of all Plain people, prohibiting electricity, telephones, and all self-propelled farm equipment. The Hoover group, now located primarily in Kentucky, continue to use horse power to thresh grain. The majority of "Pikers" and other related groups are located in Pennsylvania, Maryland and Kentucky. They number approximately 1000 adult members.

There are about 35,000 adult members of Mennonite groups that observe some Plain traditions, including dress. Old Order Mennonites that do not use tractors in the field are often referred to as "Team Mennonites." There are approximately 7000 adult members of Team Mennonite groups.

There are several other major settlements of Old Order Mennonites. The Woolwich Old Order Mennonites are located in Waterloo, Province of Ontario, and are similar to the Wenger Mennonites in practice and history. Several groups of Old Order Mennonites are located in the Rockingham County, Virginia area. The use of electricity is the major difference among these groups. In the LaGrange County, Indiana area there are several groups of Team Mennonites, and several church districts that allow automobiles.

When Old Order groups split, it is usually the case that the dissenters leave to adopt more conservative positions than the church they are leaving. Among the Amish, the major schisms in the twentieth century have found the dissenting group leaving to

adopt more liberal positions, often affiliating with a more liberal Mennonite church.

HUTTERITES

There are three Hutterite *Leut*, or peoples. These three groups did not come about as the result of a split or disagreement, but rather reflect distinct origins of the founding communities. The Dariusleut and Schmiedeleut reestablished communal living in Russia before traveling to the United States. The third Hutterite leut left Russia as individual families, but upon their arrival in South Dakota decided to established a communal settlement. This group and their descendants became known as the Lehrerleut.

The first Bruderhof colonies for all three leuts were in South Dakota. Schmiedeleut colonies are now the only Hutterite colonies left there. As well as being concentrated in South Dakota, and the province of Manitoba, there are several colonies in North Dakota and Minnesota. The Schmiedeleut are the largest of the three leut, and account for nearly forty per cent of the Hutterite population.

The Dariusleut colonies are located primarily in Canada. The province of Alberta has the largest number of such colonies, followed by Saskatchewan. There are a few colonies in Montana, and two in Washington State. The Dariusleut and Lehrerleut have almost equal populations, although the Dariusleut have more colonies, and the Lehrerleut have the larger population per colony. Lehrerleut

The early arrivals for church on Sunday are noted by their buggies. As many as thirty buggies will be assembled by the time the service begins.

Right: it takes more than bad weather to keep the horse and buggy at home.

Top right: a caravan of sleds rushes down a snowy hill. Ice hockey (far right) has become a favorite sport among the Amish.

colonies in the United States are all located in Minnesota. In Canada, there are colonies in the provinces of Alberta and Saskatchewan.

Colonies typically have between 70 and 130 people. As the population of a Bruderhof begins to near 130 people, the process of "branching" or forming a daughter colony begins. Establishing a daughter Bruderhof is a complex process. It is a business decision that requires the purchase of 3,000 to 4,000 acres of land, and a significant investment in farming equipment. It involves decisions about how the parent colony should divide itself to best establish the daughter colony without injuring the parent.

New Bruderhofs usually begin with about 60 people, who face the challenge of having more work than people to perform it. With time the new colony becomes stable, and reaches a mature stage where more land and machinery will be acquired to expand the initial holdings of the colony. Daughter colonies are usually close enough to the parent both to receive assistance and for frequent visits.

The three leuts have the same faith, much the same German dialect, and share similar work and organizational structures within their Bruderhofs. Yet there is very little marriage between those of different leuts. Leut members point out that it would be a difficult adjustment to live on a Bruderhof of a different leut because of differences in dress and custom. However, to the outside observer there seems little, if any, difference.

In 1974, a census of Hutterite Bruderhofs estimated the population to be 21,500 people. The best estimates available for 1990 suggest that there are approximately 36,500 Hutterites. The population growth is due primarily to a high birth rate and, therefore, large families. There are no efforts by the Hutterites to convert outsiders to their way of life, although from time to time outsiders do convert and become welcome members of a Hutterite Bruderhof. Like the Amish and Old Order Mennonites, the Hutterites double their population approximately every twenty years.

Previous pages: an Amish lad runs across a snow-covered field to the neighboring farm on an errand for his mother.

Only the most conservative Plain people still shuck their corn and leave it in the field until it is needed in the barn.

Left: a large hog takes a last ride to a neighboring farm to be butchered. A work "frolic" will bring several families together to share the hard physical work of butchering while enjoying the opportunity to visit.

The trip home from school becomes an occasion for a sleigh ride.

The covered bridge near Paradise, Pennsylvania.

An Amish farm is framed by the grid of an ice-covered fence.

FUTURE

Each of these Plain groups face the constant challenge of maintaining their way of life under the pressure of the modern, electronic world. Their history suggests, however, that it will take more than the challenge of the modern world to change their way of life. The Amish, Old Order Mennonites and Hutterites lose few of their children to the world. Reports on how many children are not baptized and who are lost to the church vary from fewer than five per cent to twenty per cent. The reluctance of the young to leave the community, in spite of the lure of the modern world, is a good indication of the vitality of these communities.

The future of the Plain way of life rests not on the availability of farm land, or the intrusion of government or tourist, but on the ability of these people to continue to communicate their values to their children. The success of the Plain way is based on the yielding of one's self – gelassenheit – to the community. These are values that cannot just be taught in school, or learned through instruction. The are gathered by example, and through life from childhood to the grave. The symbols of Plain life – dress, language, religion, and the horse and carriage, will mean little if not supported by the heartfelt feeling that this is the right way. And for the Plain people, there can be no doubt that it is, indeed, the right way.

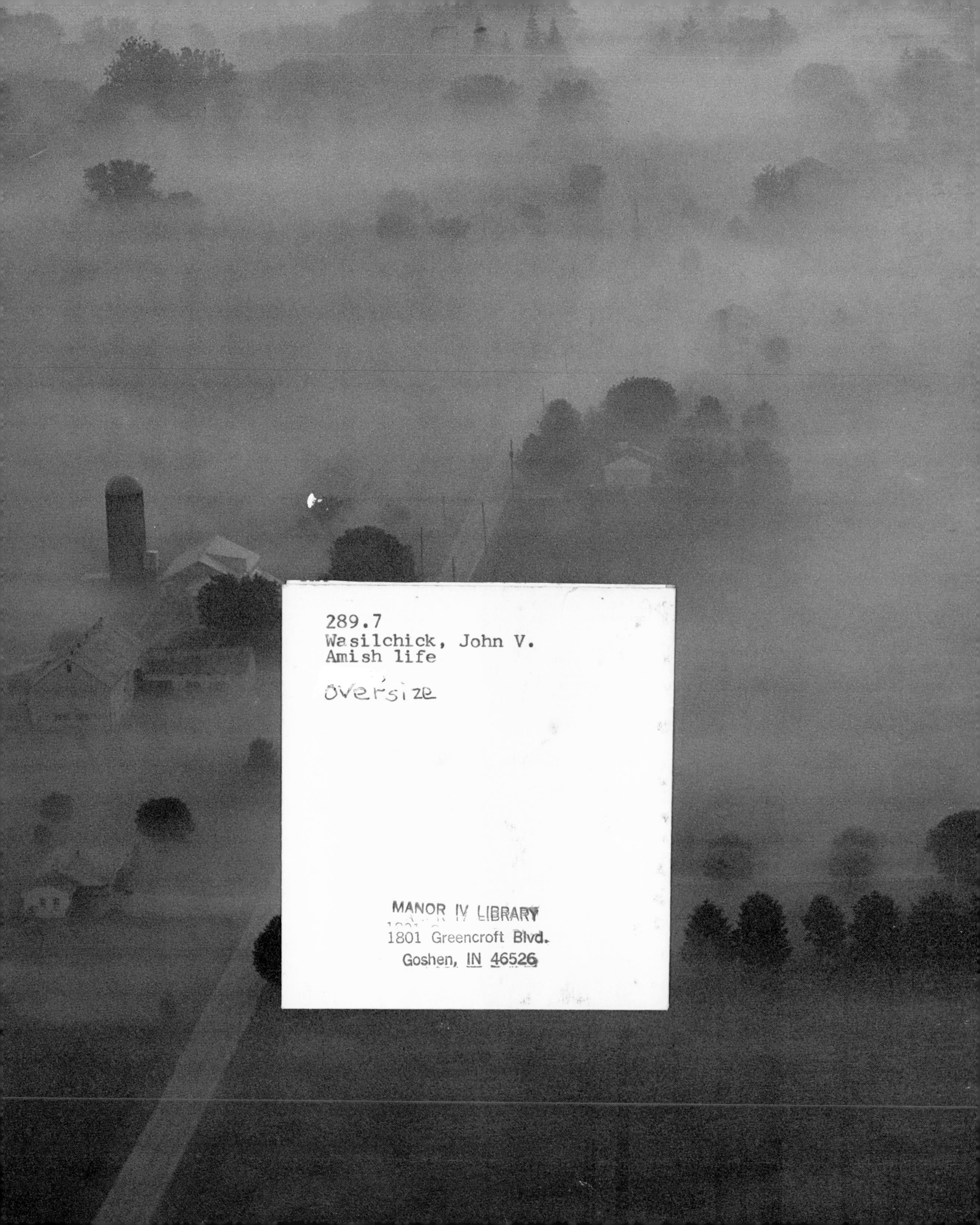